LONE STAR
FIVE STAR

THE OFFICIAL COOKBOOK OF THE
CITY OF PLANO

LONE STAR TO FIVE STAR
Culinary Creations for Every Occasion

Published by The Junior League of Plano
Copyright © 2004

The Junior League of Plano, Texas, Inc.
5805 Coit Road, Suite 301
Plano, Texas 75093
972-769-0557

Library of Congress Catalog Number: 2003104331
ISBN: 0-9720845-0-9

Edited, Designed, and Manufactured by
Favorite Recipes® Press
an imprint of

FRP™

P.O. Box 305142
Nashville, Tennessee 37230
800-358-0560

ART DIRECTOR: Steve Newman

BOOK DESIGN: Joe Warwick

FOOD PHOTOGRAPHY: Colleen Duffley

FOOD STYLISTS: Brooke Leonard and
Kathy Railsback

PROJECT MANAGER AND EDITOR: Jane Hinshaw

Printed in China
First Printing: 2004
12,500 copies
Second Printing: 2005
15,000 copies

LONE STAR
to
FIVE STAR

CULINARY CREATIONS FOR EVERY OCCASION

The Junior League of Plano

CONTENTS

FOREWORD

Did you hear about the Junior League member who thought "cooking" was a city in China? Don't be fooled by the jokes; the truth is these women can cook. The evidence is in the pages of this and hundreds of other Junior League cookbooks.

Stereotypes notwithstanding, I acquired my own admiration for the Junior League at an early age. My father, an Air Force public information officer, respected the Junior League of San Antonio as an organization whose members showed sincere interest in the military base tours he and his staff conducted for them. My mother, herself an active volunteer, was impressed by how hard the members of the Junior League worked to make our community a better place.

Is it any wonder that I eagerly accepted the opportunity to join the Junior League of Plano in 1984? Throughout all the phases of my membership I've had not a moment's regret. I couldn't begin to replace the training, the experience, and, most of all, the friendships the league has enabled me to acquire. I've told more than one group of new league members that these are the best women they'll ever meet, and I stand by that statement.

My fellow league members are also the best cooks anyone will ever encounter. A person of marginal culinary skills myself, I consider most of them to be out of my league when it comes to the kitchen. I'm always delighted, however, to partake of their offerings. A year-end committee meeting over a covered dish dinner is a guaranteed source of great eating and at least one fabulous new recipe.

Collin County is a dynamic community populated by intelligent, talented folks who work hard to ensure the best of everything for their families. Members of the Junior League of Plano take it a step further, caring about what happens beyond the boundaries of their own homes and working to ensure the best for everyone in the community.

Warm, caring, helpful, hospitable . . . these words describe the women who make up this organization. They're as busy as the day is long, but they always find time to help when help is needed. Often that help comes in the form of lovingly and skillfully prepared food. Through the ages a powerful symbol of caring and support, food sustains far more than just our bodies. Food is sustenance for our souls as well.

I reiterate: these women can cook. That they should at last publish and share their recipes is altogether fitting. And, in true Junior League fashion, they've done it right. Lots of testing and tasting are behind these pages and each recipe printed on them is exceptional.

A cookbook has been a gleam in our eyes since the Junior League of Plano was founded. Please join us in celebrating the birth of "Lone Star to Five Star."

Pasty McCutcheon

Past President, Junior League of Plano

THE JUNIOR LEAGUE

MISSION STATEMENT

The Junior League of Plano is an organization of women committed to promoting volunteerism, developing the potential of women, and improving the community through the effective action and leadership of trained volunteers. Its purpose is exclusively educational and charitable.

VISION STATEMENT

The Junior League of Plano is committed to improving family life in Collin County by promoting education and providing support to build a better community.

LEAGUE HISTORY

Established as the Plano Service League in 1976, the Junior League joined with the Association of Junior Leagues International in February 1984. Since then, The Junior League of Plano, Inc. has managed more than 200 community service projects.

PROJECTS AND INITIATIVES OF THE JUNIOR LEAGUE OF PLANO

Adolescent Sexuality Awareness Program--ASAP
BATing the Facts
Baylor Dental Mobile Unit
Camp New Horizons
Children's Pediatric Enrichment Program
CITY House, Adult Role Model
CITY House, Ready for the Real World
Collin County Council on Family Violence
Collin County Rainbow Room
Collin County Rape Crisis Center
Community Healthcare
CPR Classes
Crisis Center--ACT
Dental Care for Underprivileged Children
"Done in a Day" Volunteer Support
Drug Prevention Puppets, First Grade Drug Awareness
Eldercare Workshops
Even Start
Family Resource Library
Healthy School Initiative
Heard Natural Science Museum Outreach Program
Heritage Farmstead Docents
Hip Hip for Gray!
ITSAMONGUS
Journey of Hope
Kangaroo Krew, N.I.C.U. Family Support
Life Skills for Adolescence
Neighborhood Youth Service
Pier's Project, N.I.C.U. Family Support
Pioneer Summer Reading

Plano Acts
Plano Children's Medical Center
Plano Mother-Daughter Program
Plano War on Drugs
Project Graduation
Project LEAD
Reminiscence Program
Samaritan Inn--Touching Hearts
Sci-Tech Discovery Center
Senior Center Database
Senior Support Network
Senior Theme Dinners
Skills Workshop for Women
SOS
Substance Abuse Prevention Agency
Turning Point Teen Awareness Program
Vision Screening
Volunteer Connection
We Help Ourselves Anti-Victimization Program
Woman to Woman
Youth Mentor Network Mentor Support

THE JUNIOR LEAGUE OF PLANO SERVED AS FOUNDING PARTNER FOR THE FOLLOWING PROGRAMS:

Collin County Children's Advocacy Center
Collin County Juvenile Justice Center
Hope's Door (Collin County Women's Shelter)
Information and Referral Center
Volunteer Center of Collin County

ACKNOWLEDGMENTS

The Junior League of Plano extends special thanks to:

Central Market

Atlanta Bread Company
Chris and Doug Greenberg
Cookworks
FortyFive Ten
GourmetOnTheGo.Com
Heard-Craig House
Jason's Deli
Le Gateau, Cakery
Pottery Barn
R.S.V.P. Soiree
Tara Jones, Calligraphy
Tassels
Texas Wine and Grape Growers Association
Two Design Group
Williams Sonoma

Chefs and Restaurants:

Chong Boey, Goodhues
Bud Boswell, Blue Mesa
Central Market
Richard Chamberlain, Chamberlain's
  Steak and Chop House
Steve DeShazo, GourmetOnTheGo.Com
Dean Fearing, The Mansion
Neiman-Marcus
Maggiano's Little Italy
Patrizio's
PF Chang's China Bistro
Kent Rathbun, Abacus

The Junior League of Plano Cookbook Development Committee

CHAIR
Julie Ayres
CHAIR-ELECT
Sheri Steele
SUSTAINING ADVISORS
Sue Bond
Dee Young
RECIPE COMMITTEE
Sandi Frost, Chair
Marla Christie
Scottie Dickey
Mardi Ferrier
Teresa Loftus
Joellen Lundquest
Kimberly Nelon
Margaret Rosen
Allison Smith
Katheryn Stalker
Shawn Stratman
Beth Stubblefield

WRITING/EDITING COMMITTEE
Amy Velasquez, Chair
Tisha Harris
Kimberly Loftus
Lisa Rodenbaugh
MARKETING COMMITTEE
Kelly Hunter, Chair
Paula Adkins
Jackie Buckley
Geralyn Kaminsky
Christine Osborne
ART AND DESIGN COMMITTEE
KC Pummill, Chair
Linda McConnell
Edie Owen
Melanie Reeh
PRESIDENT
Joa Muns
PRESIDENT-ELECT
Lisa Sams
WAYS AND MEANS CHAIR
Joyce Logan

Lone Star to Five Star reflects the hard work and dedication of not only this outstanding group of women, but also their families who willingly sacrificed their time, taste buds and waistlines to help make it possible.

INTRODUCTION

Perhaps it was written in the stars that Plano, Texas, would shine as a city that is forward-thinking yet deeply traditional, fast-paced yet family-oriented, and ever expanding yet firmly established. Because of the city's terrain on the plains of Collin County, just north of Dallas, the name Plano seemed like a fitting choice when it was settled in the late 1840s. But it didn't take long for the humble name to become a bit of a misnomer, and for the thriving city to embrace more than 230,000 residents. In fact, people from over the country now call Plano home, bringing with them rich traditions to share with their new neighbors.

An "All America City," Plano boasts many bragging rights. It's been named one of the most "kid-friendly" cities in the United States and has inspired a handful of major corporations to establish their headquarters here. Our area attractions range from the down-home draw of Southfork Ranch, made famous on the television show "Dallas," to the sky-high spectacle of the Plano Balloon Festival. The Heritage Farmstead Museum transports visitors to the early days of Plano, revealing the deep-seated roots that make Plano the close-knit community it is today.

Traditions and family life run deep throughout the history of our community. McKinney, our county seat, was named in honor of pioneer Collin McKinney, a signer of the Texas Declaration of Independence. Frisco is the fastest growing city in Texas. People were originally drawn to Frisco by the railroad and fertile soil; now they are drawn by the high standard of living and new facilities, such as the new minor league ballpark which features the Frisco Rough Riders, a farm club of the Texas Rangers. Collin County is the 11th fastest growing county in the nation because it offers everything from rural charm, such as Lake Lavon, Wilson Creek Park, and the Heard Natural Science Museum and Wildlife Sanctuary, to bustling cities with thriving economies.

Family meals and celebrations are a big part of life in Collin County. With that in mind, the Junior League of Plano embarked on creating a cookbook that reflects the spirit of our city. More than 1,300 recipes were submitted--from family favorites to more fancy fare. Each was tested and tasted in our homes and at our parties, but only the most outstanding are shared in the following pages. We hope you'll delight in these dishes as much as we all do.

SAVORY CELEBRATIONS

SIP & SEE

Sip and See is a wonderful tradition here in Texas. Typically, a few friends host this shower after the baby arrives to give the proud mom a chance to show off her beautiful new baby and allow guests a peek as well. When hosting one of these joyous occasions, think of ways to turn the everyday ordinary into the extraordinary. Personalize your cookies or cake with the new baby's monogram. The mom will surely love it. You can also dress up your centerpiece by cold gluing delicate roses to a vase or bowl. You can even float one in your soup for added flair: they're edible!

menu

SHOWER PUNCH, *page 78*

STRAWBERRY SOUP, *page 107*

ROASTED PECANS, *page 62*

CHA-CHA CHICKEN SALAD, *page 99*

SUNSHINE CHEESECAKE, *page 226*

FROSTED SUGAR COOKIES, *page 213*

HARVEST
PARTY

Texans maintain a fierce pride in their football teams and often gather to cheer their teams to victory. From a local high school rivalry to the world-famous Dallas Cowboys football games, either warrants a festive Harvest Party. Write a menu to let your guests know what's in store for them, and use an old trophy as a centerpiece. Pack raffia-tied bags of goodies, such as spiced pecans, to enjoy during the game. Also, keep your team colors in mind when decorating, and your party is sure to score with all of your football friends!

menu

TEXAS BEER

SWISS FONDUE, *page 71*

TEXAS CHILI, *page 114*

BLUE CORN MUFFINS, *page 53*

PRALINE PUMPKIN TORTE, *page 201*

Game Day

Spinach Artichoke Dip
Savory Fondue
Chili
Jalapeño Corn Muffins
Pumpkin Tart
Pecan Pork

TEXAS BARBECUE

Few things go hand in hand like Texas and barbecue. There is something about Texas' rough-and-tumble image and down-home friendly hospitality that makes Texas and barbecue a perfect fit. Barbecues are often planned at a moment's notice, so simplify entertaining. Think rustic by using an old milk pitcher filled with sunflowers as your centerpiece, and serve barbecue sauce from empty coke bottles. Keep the atmosphere festive with candles and music. Enjoy and celebrate any occasion with a barbecue, and be sure to invite many friends.

BALLOON FESTIVAL
PICNIC

The Plano Balloon Festival attracts more than 100,000 visitors each year and is Texas' largest hot air balloon event. If you are attending a special festival in your area or just visiting a local park, pack a picnic. Old-fashioned simplicity makes for some of the most charming of picnics. For instance, serve potato salad from a canning jar and wrap sandwiches in butcher paper tied with raffia ribbon. And don't forget that picnics are all about rest and relaxation. So pack some throw pillows, find a shady spot, and let the natural beauty surround you with easy entertainment!

menu

FRIENDS

Show your friends how special they are by inviting them over for a quiet evening at home. Create the perfect ambiance by having a cozy fire in the hearth or by placing candles throughout the room. Serve your wine from tumblers for a European flair and use an antique knife for cheese service. An iron grate placed on your tablecloth will add dimension and layering to your table. And don't forget to add that special touch with a flower folded into each napkin.

menu

HOLIDAY
PARTY

menu

GOLDEN WASSAIL, *page 81*

STUFFED MUSHROOMS, *page 60*

WINTER SALAD, *page 93*

CROWN ROAST OF PORK WITH CRANBERRY SAUSAGE STUFFING, *page 133*

BROCCOLI TIMBALES, *page 170*

SWEET POTATO SOUFFLÉ, *page 175*

POACHED PEARS WITH RASPBERRY SAUCE, *page 223*

The holidays are perhaps the most special time of year, made even more memorable by the celebrations you host for family and friends. Creating a beautifully inviting table is a great way to set the tone. For starters, anchor your table with a dramatic floral arrangement, selecting different flowers in the same color family, such as a deep shade of red. To soften the look and add ambiance, place votive candles in groups of three around the table. For a personal touch, set place cards by each plate to let your guests know they have a special place at your celebration.

RISING STARS

BLUE MESA EGGS BENEDICT

Bud Boswell, Executive Chef at Blue Mesa Grill, serves up Southwestern fare that's been lauded by food critics around North Texas. If you ask Blue Mesa's legions of loyal customers, they will tell you the Sunday brunch is not to be missed.

Cilantro Béarnaise

1/4	cup white wine
3	tablespoons chopped cilantro
1	tablespoon finely chopped onion
2	cups (4 sticks) butter
3	egg yolks
	juice of 1/2 lemon
1/4	to 1/2 teaspoon Tabasco sauce

Poached Eggs

2	quarts water
2	tablespoons white vinegar
8	eggs

Assembly

4	English muffins, split and toasted
8	(1-ounce) slices Canadian bacon, grilled
4	black olives, cut into halves
	paprika to taste

To prepare the béarnaise, combine the wine with the cilantro and onion in a saucepan. Cook over medium-high heat for 2 minutes or until reduced by half, stirring constantly. Remove from the heat. Place the butter in a microwave-safe dish and microwave on High until melted and bubbly.

Combine the egg yolks, lemon juice and Tabasco sauce in a double boiler and mix well. Cook over simmering water until thickened, whisking constantly. Add the melted butter gradually, whisking until smooth. Add a small amount of cold water if the mixture appears too thick. Whisk in the cilantro and wine mixture. Keep warm.

To poach the eggs, bring the water to a simmer or just until bubbles form around the edge in a saucepan. Stir in the vinegar. Crack the eggs carefully into the water 1 at a time, keeping separated with a slotted spoon. Cook until done to taste and remove with the slotted spoon. Drain.

To assemble the dish, place the toasted English muffins on serving plates. Top each muffin half with a slice of Canadian bacon and a poached egg. Spoon the béarnaise over the eggs and garnish with a black olive. Sprinkle with paprika to serve.
Serves four

GOODHUES BAKED SALMON IN BURGUNDY SAUCE WITH ORANGE ONION MARMALADE

The baked salmon brunch entrée is one of Executive Chef Chong Boey's specialties. Formerly with the French Room and Jennivines, both in Dallas, Chef Chong brought his expertise to Goodhues Wood-Fired Grill in historic downtown McKinney.

Orange Onion Marmalade

1/4	cup (1/2 stick) unsalted butter
2	onions, sliced
1	teaspoon grated orange zest
1	tablespoon slivered basil
1	cup burgundy
1/4	cup sugar
	salt and pepper to taste

Salmon and Burgundy Sauce

4	(8-ounce) boneless salmon fillets
1	cup burgundy
1	cup cream
	salt and pepper to taste

To prepare the marmalade, melt the butter in a large skillet over high heat. Add the onion slices and cook for 10 minutes or until caramelized, stirring frequently. Add the orange zest and basil. Stir in the wine and sugar. Cook until most of the liquid has evaporated. Season with salt and pepper and cool slightly.

To prepare the salmon and sauce, place the salmon fillets in a baking dish and add the wine and cream. Sprinkle with salt and pepper. Bake at 450 degrees for 8 minutes. Remove the salmon to serving plates. Pour the cooking juices into a saucepan. Cook until reduced to a syrup consistency. Adjust the seasoning.

Spoon the marmalade onto each salmon fillet. Spoon the sauce over the top and serve immediately.

Serves four

CHEFS' RECIPES

MINTED FRUIT SALAD

1	medium cantaloupe
1	medium honeydew melon
1	pint strawberries, stemmed
3	kiwifruit, peeled and sliced
1/2	cup finely chopped mint leaves
1/2	cup fresh orange juice
1/4	cup fresh lemon juice
3	tablespoons sugar

Cut the cantaloupe and honeydew melon into balls with a melon baller. Combine with the strawberries and kiwifruit in a large bowl and mix gently. Sprinkle with the mint. Combine the orange juice, lemon juice and sugar in a small bowl and mix well. Pour over the fruit and toss to coat well. Chill in the refrigerator for 2 to 3 hours. Serve chilled.
Serves twelve

ORANGE SUNSHINE

4	eggs, beaten
1	cup half-and-half
1	cup orange juice
1/8	teaspoon grated orange zest
3/4	cup sugar
1/2	teaspoon vanilla extract
1/8	teaspoon nutmeg
2	teaspoons butter
	orange slices

Combine the eggs, half-and-half, orange juice, orange zest, sugar, vanilla and nutmeg in a saucepan and mix well. Cook over low heat for 5 minutes or until thickened, stirring constantly. Remove from the heat and stir in the butter until melted. Pour into individual fruit cups and chill for 2 to 8 hours. Garnish with orange slices.
Serves four to six

PINEAPPLE SPREAD *with crackers is a nice accompaniment for fruit. Combine 16 ounces softened cream cheese, 1 drained small can of crushed pineapple, 3/4 cup toasted pecans, and 3/4 cup sliced green onions in a bowl and mix well. Chill, covered, for 1 hour or longer. Let stand until room temperature to serve. Serve with crackers or use as a sandwich spread.*

BACON AND TOMATO TARTLETS

1	(8-count) can flaky biscuits
6	slices bacon, crisp-fried, drained and crumbled
1	medium tomato, seeded and chopped
3/4	cup (3 ounces) shredded mozzarella cheese
1/2	cup mayonnaise
1	teaspoon basil leaves
1	teaspoon thyme
1/2	teaspoon oregano
3/4	teaspoon garlic salt

Pull the layers of each biscuit apart to form three pieces. Press into muffin cups lightly sprayed with nonstick cooking spray. Combine the bacon, tomato, mozzarella cheese, mayonnaise, basil, thyme, oregano and garlic salt in a bowl and mix well. Spoon into the prepared muffin cups. Bake at 375 degrees for 10 to 12 minutes or until golden brown.
Makes twenty-four

BOURSIN BAKED EGGS

4	teaspoons unsalted butter
1/4	cup heavy cream
4	eggs
4	teaspoons crumbled herbed boursin cheese
	freshly ground pepper to taste

Place 1 teaspoon butter and 2 teaspoons of the cream in each of four 3/4-cup baking ramekins. Break 1 egg into the center of each ramekin. Place 1 teaspoon boursin cheese on each egg and top with 1 teaspoon cream. Sprinkle with pepper.

Place the ramekins in a baking dish and add enough water to reach halfway up the sides of the ramekins. Bake at 450 degrees for 7 to 10 minutes or until the egg yolks are set. Serve immediately.
Serves four

The photograph for this recipe is on page 25.

HUEVOS CON PAPAS

2	tablespoons butter or vegetable oil
1/4	cup chopped onion
1/4	cup chopped green or red bell pepper (optional)
2	cups chopped cooked potatoes or frozen cubed potatoes
1/2	to 1 cup salsa
6	to 8 eggs, lightly beaten
1	cup crumbled crisp-fried bacon, crumbled cooked sausage or chopped cooked ham (optional)
1	cup (4 ounces) shredded Cheddar cheese, Monterey Jack cheese or pepper Jack cheese

Heat the butter in a skillet and add the onion, bell pepper and potatoes. Sauté until the potatoes are golden brown and the onion is translucent. Stir in the salsa.

Pour the eggs over the potato mixture in the skillet and cook until the eggs are set on the bottom. Stir gently through the eggs with a spatula and continue to cook until the eggs are soft set; do not overmix. Add the bacon and cheese. Serve immediately with additional salsa. You may also serve rolled in warmed corn tortillas.

For Huevos con Migas, add torn corn tortillas to the eggs; it's a delicious way to use stale tortillas.

Serves four

EASY CHEESE SOUFFLÉ

6	eggs
1	cup heavy cream
1/4	teaspoon nutmeg
1	teaspoon salt
	pepper to taste
2	cups (8 ounces) shredded Cheddar cheese
1/2	cup (2 ounces) grated Parmesan cheese

Beat the eggs in a mixing bowl. Add the cream, nutmeg, salt and pepper and mix well. Fold in the Cheddar cheese and Parmesan cheese. Spoon into a greased baking dish. Bake at 425 degrees for 45 minutes or until set and golden brown.

Serves six

GREEN CHILE STRATA

1	loaf French bread
1 1/2	cups (6 ounces) shredded Monterey Jack cheese
1 1/2	cups (6 ounces) shredded Cheddar cheese
8	ounces cream cheese, chopped
8	slices bacon, crisp-fried and crumbled
3	to 5 roasted fresh green chiles, peeled, seeded and chopped
10	eggs
2	cups milk
1/2	teaspoon dry mustard
	cayenne pepper to taste

Cut the crust from the French bread and tear the bread into pieces. Spread in a greased 9×13-inch baking dish. Layer the Monterey Jack cheese, Cheddar cheese and cream cheese over the bread. Top with the bacon and green chiles.

Beat the eggs in a bowl and stir in the milk, dry mustard and cayenne pepper. Pour over the layers. Bake at 350 degrees for 55 to 60 minutes or until set and golden brown. Let stand for 10 minutes before serving.

Serves eight

PICO DE GALLO *will spice up a breakfast dish. Mix 2 cups chopped fresh tomatoes, 1/2 cup chopped onion, 1 finely chopped jalapeño pepper, 2 to 3 tablespoons chopped cilantro, and the juice of 1 or 2 limes in a bowl. Season with salt and pepper. Store in the refrigerator for 8 hours or longer to blend the flavors. You may also add fresh fruit such as peaches, watermelon, or pineapple.*

VEGETABLE FRITTATA

8	slices white bread, cubed
1/4	cup vegetable oil
1	purple onion, sliced
2	red bell peppers, cut into thin strips
1	yellow bell pepper, cut into thin strips
2	yellow squash, thinly sliced
2	zucchini, thinly sliced
8	ounces mushrooms, sliced
3	garlic cloves, minced
6	eggs
1/4	cup heavy cream
2 1/2	teaspoons salt
2	teaspoons pepper
2	cups (8 ounces) shredded Swiss cheese
8	ounces cream cheese, cubed

Spread half the bread cubes in a lightly greased 9×13-inch baking dish. Heat the vegetable oil in a large skillet. Add the onion, bell peppers, yellow squash, zucchini, mushrooms and garlic and sauté until the vegetables are tender. Remove to paper towels to drain and pat dry.

Beat the eggs with the cream in a mixing bowl and add the remaining bread cubes, salt and pepper; mix well. Stir in the sautéed vegetables, Swiss cheese and cream cheese. Pour into the prepared baking dish.

Bake at 325 degrees for 45 minutes. Cover with foil to prevent overbrowning and bake for 15 minutes longer or until set.

Serves ten to twelve

CRUSTLESS HAM AND GRITS QUICHE

1/2	cup water
1/4	teaspoon salt
1/3	cup uncooked quick-cooking yellow grits
1	(12-ounce) can evaporated milk
1 1/2	cups chopped cooked ham
1	cup (4 ounces) shredded sharp Cheddar cheese
1	tablespoon chopped fresh parsley
1	to 2 teaspoons hot sauce
3	eggs, lightly beaten

Bring the water and salt to a boil in a large saucepan. Stir in the grits. Remove from the heat and let stand for 5 minutes; the mixture will be thick. Stir in the evaporated milk, ham, cheese, parsley, hot sauce and eggs.

Spoon into a lightly greased 9 1/2-inch quiche dish or deep-dish pie plate. Bake at 350 degrees for 30 to 35 minutes or until set and golden brown. Let stand for 10 minutes before serving.

Serves four to six

VEGETARIAN QUICHE

Quiche Pastry

2	cups sifted flour
1	teaspoon kosher salt
1	teaspoon freshly ground pepper
3/4	cup shortening
5	tablespoons (or more) ice water

Filling

12	eggs
2	cups heavy cream
6	drops of Tabasco sauce
1	teaspoon chopped fresh basil
1	teaspoon chopped fresh oregano
1	teaspoon chopped fresh rosemary
2	teaspoons kosher salt
1/2	teaspoon freshly ground pepper
1	cup sliced mushrooms, roasted
4	Roma tomatoes, sliced and roasted
2	red onions, sliced and roasted
2	tablespoons chopped roasted garlic
1	(16-ounce) can artichoke hearts, drained
1/3	cup sliced black olives
2 1/2	cups (10 ounces) shredded mozzarella cheese
1	cup (4 ounces) grated Parmesan cheese

To prepare the pastry, mix the flour, kosher salt and pepper in a mixing bowl. Cut in the shortening until crumbly. Add the ice water 1 tablespoon at a time, mixing to form a dough. Shape the dough into a ball and wrap with plastic wrap. Let rest in the refrigerator for 1 hour or longer.

Roll the dough into a circle 1/8 inch thick on a floured surface. Fit into a springform pan, allowing the dough to drape over the side of the pan. Store in the refrigerator until time to fill.

To prepare the filling, combine the eggs, cream, Tabasco sauce, basil, oregano, rosemary, kosher salt and pepper in a mixing bowl and whisk until smooth. Stir in the mushrooms, tomatoes, red onions, garlic, artichoke hearts, black olives, mozzarella cheese and Parmesan cheese. Spoon into the prepared springform pan. Bake at 325 degrees for 1 1/2 hours or until set. Serve warm.

Serves six to eight

BLUE CHEESE GRITS

3	cups milk
1	garlic clove, minced
1¹/₄	teaspoons salt
1	cup uncooked quick-cooking grits
¹/₂	to 1 cup (2 to 4 ounces) crumbled blue cheese
¹/₂	cup heavy cream
2	eggs, lightly beaten
2	egg whites, lightly beaten
¹/₃	cup chopped butter
1	(4-ounce) can chopped green chiles
2	tablespoons grated Parmesan cheese
2	teaspoons chopped fresh basil
1	teaspoon chopped fresh thyme

Combine the milk, garlic and salt in a medium saucepan and bring to a boil. Stir in the grits and reduce the heat. Cook, covered, using the directions on the grits package. Remove from the heat and whisk in the blue cheese until melted.

Add the cream, eggs, egg whites, butter, green chiles, Parmesan cheese, basil and thyme and mix well. Spoon into a greased baking dish. Bake at 325 degrees for 1 hour or until set.
Serves six

USE **FRESH FLOWERS** *as the centerpiece for your next brunch celebration. For added flair, slice apples into rounds, fill the vase with water, and arrange the apple slices around the side of the vase before adding the flowers. Use your imagination; the possibilities are endless.*

Sausage Filling

1/4   cup chopped onion
1   pound bulk hot or mild sausage
1/2   cup (2 ounces) shredded Cheddar cheese
3   ounces cream cheese

Crepes

1   cup sifted unbleached flour
1/4   teaspoon salt
2   eggs, beaten
1 1/4   cups low-fat milk or water
     unsalted butter

Dill Sauce

1/2   cup (4 ounces) sour cream
2   tablespoons butter, softened
     dillweed to taste

To prepare the filling, sauté the onion in a large nonstick skillet for 1 minute. Add the sausage and cook until brown and crumbly, stirring frequently; drain. Combine with the Cheddar cheese and cream cheese in a large bowl and mix until the cheeses melt.

To prepare the crepes, sift the flour and salt in a large bowl. Whisk the eggs with 1 cup of the milk in a bowl. Add to the flour and whisk until smooth. Add enough of the remaining 1/4 cup milk or water if needed to make a thin batter.

Coat a griddle or 7-inch skillet with unsalted butter and heat over medium-high heat until sizzling. Ladle 2 tablespoons of the crepe batter at a time onto the griddle and tilt to coat the bottom evenly. Cook for 1 to 2 minutes or until the edge begins to curl from the pan; slide onto a plate. Repeat the process with the remaining ingredients, adding butter as needed and stacking the crepes as they are cooked.

Spoon the filling onto the crepes and roll to enclose the filling. Arrange in a greased baking dish. Chill, covered, for 1 hour or longer. Bake, uncovered, at 350 degrees for 35 minutes.

To prepare the sauce, combine the sour cream, butter and dillweed in a bowl and mix well. Spread over the crepes and bake for 5 minutes longer.

Serves eight to ten

Breakfast Cake

1	pound pork sausage
2	cups flour
1	teaspoon baking powder
1/2	teaspoon baking soda
1/2	cup (1 stick) butter, softened
3/4	cup sugar
1/4	cup packed brown sugar
2	eggs
1	cup (8 ounces) sour cream
1	cup blueberries
1/2	cup pecans (optional)

Blueberry Sauce

1/2	cup sugar
1/2	cup water
2	tablespoons cornstarch
2	cups blueberries
1/2	teaspoon lemon juice

To prepare the cake, cook the sausage in a skillet, stirring until brown and crumbly; drain. Mix the flour, baking powder and baking soda together. Cream the butter in a mixing bowl until light. Add the sugar and brown sugar and beat until fluffy. Add the eggs 1 at a time, beating for 1 minute after each addition. Add the flour mixture alternately with the sour cream, beating just until moistened after each addition.

Fold the sausage, blueberries and pecans into the batter. Spoon into an ungreased 9×13-inch baking pan. Bake at 350 degrees for 35 to 40 minutes or until the cake tests done.

To prepare the sauce, combine the sugar, water and cornstarch in a saucepan and mix well. Stir in the blueberries. Cook over medium heat until thick and bubbly, stirring constantly. Cook for 2 minutes longer. Stir in the lemon juice.

Cut the cake into squares and serve with the sauce. Store the leftover portions of both the cake and sauce in the refrigerator.

Serves twelve

FROZEN STRAWBERRY DELIGHT

1	cup sifted flour
1/4	cup packed brown sugar
1/2	cup chopped pecans or walnuts
1/2	cup (1 stick) butter, melted
2	egg whites
1	cup sugar
2	cups sliced strawberries
2	tablespoons lemon juice
1	cup whipping cream, whipped
	whole strawberries and mint leaves

Mix the flour, brown sugar and pecans in a bowl. Add the butter and mix until crumbly. Spread the mixture in a baking pan. Toast at 350 degrees for 20 minutes, stirring occasionally. Press 2/3 of the crumb mixture into a 9×13-inch baking pan.

Combine the egg whites, sugar, sliced strawberries and lemon juice in a large mixing bowl. Beat at high speed for 10 minutes. Spoon into the prepared pan and top with the remaining crumb mixture.

Freeze for 6 hours or longer. Cut into squares and place on serving plates. Top with the whipped cream and garnish with whole strawberries and mint leaves.
Serves twelve

YORKSHIRE PUDDING

	beef roast drippings
1	cup sifted flour
1/4	teaspoon salt
3	eggs
1	cup milk

Remove 3 tablespoons of beef drippings from the pan in which a beef roast is roasting about 20 minutes before the roast is ready. Place 1/2 teaspoon of the drippings in each of 9 muffin cups. Place in a 400 degree oven to heat.

Sift the flour and salt together. Process the eggs in a food processor or blender until well mixed. Add the sifted ingredients gradually, processing constantly. Drizzle in the milk and process for 2 minutes.

Spoon the batter into the heated muffin cups, filling 1/2 to 2/3 full. Bake at 400 degrees for 12 to 14 minutes or until golden brown. Serve with roast beef.
Makes nine

ANGEL BISCUITS

1	envelope dry yeast
2	tablespoons lukewarm water
5	cups flour
1	tablespoon baking powder
1	teaspoon baking soda
2	tablespoons sugar
1 1/2	teaspoons salt
1	cup shortening
2	cups buttermilk
	melted butter

Dissolve the yeast in the lukewarm water in a cup. Sift the flour, baking powder, baking soda, sugar and salt into a large bowl. Cut in the shortening with a pastry blender until the mixture is crumbly. Add the buttermilk and yeast mixture and mix until moistened.

Knead briefly on a floured surface. Roll 1/2 inch thick and cut into rounds. Brush with melted butter and place on an ungreased baking sheet. Bake at 400 degrees for 12 to 15 minutes or until golden brown.
Makes thirty

BISCUITS WITH GRAVY *is a favorite treat combination found on breakfast tables in North Texas. If you have not tried this simple southern delight, just prepare Angel Biscuits (above) and serve them with Creamy White Gravy. To make the gravy, reserve 2 to 3 tablespoons of bacon or sausage drippings in the skillet and stir in an equal amount of flour. Cook over medium heat for about 5 minutes. Stir in 1 cup milk gradually and bring to a boil, stirring constantly. Add more milk if needed for the desired consistency. Season with salt and pepper. This is also a great way to recycle biscuits left from an evening meal.*

Biscuits

1	cup whipping cream
1 1/2	cups flour
4	teaspoons baking powder
1/2	teaspoon salt
2	tablespoons melted butter
1/2	cup packed light brown sugar
2	tablespoons ground cinnamon

Pecan Topping

1/2	cup packed light brown sugar
2	tablespoons heavy cream
1/2	cup finely chopped pecans
1	teaspoon vanilla extract
1/2	teaspoon butter pecan extract

To prepare the biscuits, whip the cream in a chilled mixing bowl until soft peaks form. Whisk together the flour, baking powder and salt. Add the flour mixture to the whipped cream gradually and mix with a rubber spatula to form a stiff dough.

Knead the dough on a floured surface for 1 minute. Roll into a 9×12-inch rectangle 1/4 inch thick. Brush with the melted butter and sprinkle evenly with the brown sugar and cinnamon.

Roll up from the long side to enclose the brown sugar and cinnamon. Cut into slices with a serrated knife. Place the slices close together in a greased 8-inch baking pan. Bake at 425 degrees for 15 minutes or until golden brown.

To prepare the topping, combine the brown sugar, cream, pecans and flavorings in a bowl and mix well. Spread over the cinnamon biscuits and bake for 3 to 4 minutes longer or until the topping is bubbly.

Serves four

BASIL AND TOMATO DROP BISCUITS

1/2	cup finely chopped onion
1	tablespoon olive oil
3/4	cup finely chopped tomato
1/4	cup chopped fresh basil
1/2	teaspoon dried oregano
2	cups flour
1	tablespoon baking powder
1	teaspoon salt
1/2	teaspoon pepper
1/3	cup shortening
2/3	cup milk

Sauté the onion in the olive oil in a skillet until tender. Add the tomato and sauté for 1 minute longer. Stir in the basil and oregano and remove from the heat. Cool slightly.

Mix the flour, baking powder, salt and pepper in a large bowl. Cut in the shortening until the mixture resembles coarse crumbs. Add the milk and the tomato mixture and mix just until moistened; the dough will be sticky. Drop by spoonfuls onto an ungreased baking sheet. Bake at 425 degrees for 10 to 12 minutes or until golden brown.

Makes twenty-four

THANKSGIVING ROLLS

1/2	cup (1 stick) butter or margarine, softened
1	cup (8 ounces) sour cream
1/2	cup sugar
1	teaspoon salt
2	envelopes dry yeast
1/2	cup lukewarm water
2	eggs
4	cups flour
2	to 4 tablespoons melted butter

Combine the softened butter, sour cream, sugar and salt in a saucepan. Cook over medium-low heat until the butter melts, stirring to blend well. Cool to lukewarm. Sprinkle the yeast over the lukewarm water in a 1-cup measure and let stand for 5 minutes. Combine the sour cream mixture, yeast mixture, eggs and flour in a large bowl and mix until moistened; do not beat. Store, covered, in the refrigerator for 8 hours.

Divide the dough into 4 portions and shape into balls. Roll each portion 1/4 inch thick on a floured surface and cut into 2-inch circles. Brush each circle evenly with the melted butter and fold over into half-circles; press lightly to seal. Arrange with sides touching in a 10×15-inch baking pan.

Cover lightly with a towel and let rise in a warm place for 45 minutes or until doubled in bulk. Bake at 375 degrees for 12 to 15 minutes or until golden brown.

Makes four dozen

1 1/2   teaspoons dry yeast
2   tablespoons warm water
1/2   cup milk
1/2   cup (1 stick) butter
1/2   teaspoon salt
1/3   cup sugar
2 1/4   cups flour
1   egg, lightly beaten
1   cup sugar
1/2   cup packed light brown sugar
1   tablespoon cinnamon
6   tablespoons (3/4 stick) butter, melted

Dissolve the yeast in the warm water in a cup. Scald the milk in a saucepan. Add the butter and stir until the butter melts. Pour the mixture into a bowl and stir in the salt and 1/3 cup sugar until dissolved. Add the yeast mixture and 1 cup of the flour and beat until smooth. Add the egg and beat for 2 minutes. Add 1 cup flour and mix well; then add the remaining flour and mix until a dough forms.

Knead very lightly 8 times on a floured surface. Place in a greased bowl, turning to coat the surface. Let rise until doubled in bulk. Remove to a floured surface and roll into an 8×10-inch rectangle.

Mix 1 cup sugar, brown sugar and cinnamon in a bowl; reserve 3/4 cup of the mixture for the topping. Brush the dough with 1 tablespoon of the melted butter and sprinkle with the remaining cinnamon mixture. Roll the dough from the long side to enclose the cinnamon mixture. Cut into 24 slices.

Spread the remaining 5 tablespoons butter in a 7×10-inch baking pan. Arrange the roll slices cut side up in the pan, pressing down to force the butter up around the slices. Sprinkle with the reserved cinnamon mixture and press down again. Let rise until doubled in bulk.

Bake the rolls at 375 degrees for 20 minutes or until golden brown. Serve warm.
Makes twenty-four

Braids

1	cup (8 ounces) sour cream
1/2	cup sugar
1	teaspoon salt
1/2	cup (1 stick) butter, melted
2	envelopes dry yeast
1/2	cup warm water
2	eggs, beaten
4	cups flour
16	ounces cream cheese, softened
3/4	cup sugar
1	egg
1/8	teaspoon salt
2	teaspoons vanilla extract

Confectioners' Sugar Glaze

2	cups confectioners' sugar
1/4	cup milk
2	teaspoons vanilla extract

To prepare the braids, heat the sour cream in a small saucepan over low heat. Stir in 1/2 cup sugar, 1 teaspoon salt and the melted butter. Remove from the heat and cool to lukewarm.

Sprinkle the yeast over the warm water in a large mixing bowl and stir to dissolve. Add the sour cream mixture, 2 eggs and flour and mix to form a smooth dough. Store, tightly covered, in the refrigerator for 8 to 12 hours.

Combine the cream cheese and 3/4 cup sugar in a small mixing bowl and beat until light and fluffy. Add 1 egg, 1/8 teaspoon salt and the vanilla and mix well.

Divide the dough into 4 equal portions. Roll each portion into an 8×12-inch rectangle on a floured surface. Spread each rectangle with 1/4 of the cream cheese mixture. Roll each from the long side to enclose the cream cheese filling; press the edges and fold under the ends slightly.

Place the rolls seam side down on greased 10×15-inch baking sheets. Cut diagonally 1/3 of the way through the rolls at 2-inch intervals to resemble braids. Let rise, covered, in a warm place for 1 hour or until doubled in bulk. Bake at 375 degrees for 15 to 20 minutes or until golden brown.

To prepare the glaze, combine the confectioners' sugar, milk and vanilla in a small mixing bowl and mix until smooth. Spread over the warm braids.

Serves twenty-eight to thirty

Coffee Cake

1¹/2	cups flour
1	teaspoon baking powder
¹/2	teaspoon salt
¹/2	cup (1 stick) butter, softened
¹/2	cup sugar
2	eggs
1	cup (8 ounces) sour cream
2	teaspoons grated lemon zest
1	teaspoon vanilla extract

Coffee Cake Topping

1	pint blueberries
¹/2	cup chopped pecans
¹/4	cup sugar
1	teaspoon cinnamon

Coffee Cake Glaze

1	cup confectioners' sugar
4	teaspoons milk

To prepare the coffee cake, mix the flour, baking powder and salt together. Cream the butter in a mixing bowl until light. Add the sugar gradually and beat for 2 to 3 minutes or until fluffy. Add the eggs, sour cream, lemon zest and vanilla and beat until smooth. Add the flour mixture gradually and mix well. Spoon into a lightly greased 9-inch springform pan.

To prepare the topping, crush ¹/4 cup of the blueberries in a bowl. Add the remaining blueberries, pecans, sugar and cinnamon and mix gently. Sprinkle over the batter.

Bake at 350 degrees for 35 to 40 minutes or until a wooden pick inserted into the center comes out clean. Cool in the pan for 10 to 15 minutes. Place on a serving plate and remove the side of the pan.

To prepare the glaze, whisk the confectioners' sugar and milk in a bowl until smooth. Drizzle over the coffee cake.

Serves eight

FRENCH TOAST WITH APPLE SYRUP

French Toast

1/2	cup (1 stick) butter
1	cup packed brown sugar
2	tablespoons corn syrup
2	Granny Smith apples, peeled and thinly sliced
1	loaf French bread, sliced 3/4 inch thick
5	eggs
1 1/2	cups milk
1	teaspoon vanilla extract
1	teaspoon nutmeg

Apple Syrup

1	cup applesauce
1	(10-ounce) jar apple jelly
1/2	teaspoon cinnamon
1/8	teaspoon ground cloves
	salt to taste

To prepare the toast, combine the butter, brown sugar and corn syrup in a small saucepan. Cook over low heat until the butter melts and the sugar dissolves. Pour into a 9×13-inch baking dish. Arrange the apple slices in the dish and layer the bread over the apples.

Combine the eggs, milk, vanilla and nutmeg in a mixing bowl and whisk until smooth. Pour over the bread. Chill, covered with plastic wrap, for 8 to 12 hours. Bake at 350 degrees for 40 minutes.

To prepare the syrup, combine the applesauce, apple jelly, cinnamon, cloves and salt in a small saucepan. Cook over medium heat until the mixture is heated through, stirring constantly until smooth. Serve with the French toast.

Serves eight

A SMOOTHIE *with strawberries and bananas is enjoyable for breakfast or a nutritious snack. Combine 6 ounces of yogurt, 4 large strawberries, 1 chopped banana, 1 tablespoon sugar, and 1/2 cup orange juice or other fruit juice in a blender and process until smooth. Serve in a glass garnished with mint or a strawberry. You may substitute other fruits, such as blueberries or peaches, for the strawberries and/or banana.*

CLASSIC FRENCH TOAST

3   eggs
1¹/2   cups milk
1   tablespoon sugar
1   teaspoon vanilla extract (optional)
1   tablespoon cinnamon (optional)
       salt to taste
       melted butter or vegetable oil
8   slices thickly sliced bread

Beat the eggs lightly in a mixing bowl. Add the milk, sugar, vanilla, cinnamon and salt and mix well. Heat a griddle over medium heat and brush with butter.

Dip the bread in the egg mixture and place on the griddle. Cook until golden brown on the bottom. Turn the bread over and cook until golden brown. Serve with Blueberry Sauce, syrup, butter or fresh fruit.

Serves four

BLUEBERRY SAUCE

1   tablespoon cornstarch
1   tablespoon water
2   cups blueberries
¹/2   cup sugar
¹/2   cup water
       fresh lemon juice to taste

Blend the cornstarch and 1 tablespoon water in a cup. Combine with the blueberries, sugar and ¹/2 cup water in a small saucepan. Cook over medium heat until the blueberries are tender and the mixture thickens. Stir in the lemon juice. Serve over French toast, ice cream or pound cake.

Makes two cups

GERMAN PANCAKE

1	cup milk
2	tablespoons sugar
2	eggs
2/3	cup flour
1	teaspoon vanilla extract
1/2	teaspoon salt
1/4	cup (1/2 stick) butter

Combine the milk, sugar, eggs, flour, vanilla and salt in a blender and blend until smooth. Place the butter in a round 9-inch baking pan. Place in a 400-degree oven until the butter melts. Pour the batter into the prepared pan.

Bake at 400 degrees for 30 to 35 minutes or until brown and puffy; the center will be moist and custard-like. Cut into wedges and serve with confectioners' sugar and lemon.

Serves four

BREAKFAST POPOVER

1/4	cup (1/2 stick) butter
1/2	cup milk
2	eggs
1/2	cup flour
	juice of 1 or 2 lemons
	confectioners' sugar

Place the butter in a 10-inch cast-iron skillet. Place in a 475-degree oven for 5 minutes or until the butter melts.

Combine the milk and eggs in a blender and blend until smooth. Add the flour and mix well. Pour into the prepared skillet. Bake at 475 degrees for 12 minutes. Squeeze the lemon juice over the hot popover and sprinkle with confectioners' sugar. Serve immediately.

You may prepare the batter in advance and store in the refrigerator for 8 to 12 hours before baking. Double the recipe to prepare in a 12-inch skillet.

Serves four

Pastry

1/2	cup (1 stick) butter
1	cup flour
2	tablespoons water
1/2	cup (1 stick) butter
1	cup water
1	teaspoon almond extract
1	cup flour
3	eggs

Confectioners' Sugar Frosting

1/4	cup (1/2 stick) butter
1	(1-pound) package confectioners' sugar
1	tablespoon (about) milk
1	teaspoon almond extract or vanilla extract
	slivered almonds

To prepare the pastry, cut 1/2 cup butter into 1 cup flour in a bowl until crumbly. Sprinkle with 2 tablespoons water and mix with a fork to form a dough. Shape into 2 balls and pat into two 3×12-inch strips on an ungreased baking sheet.

Combine 1/2 cup butter and 1 cup water in a small saucepan and bring to a rolling boil. Add the almond extract and remove from the heat. Add 1 cup flour immediately, stirring until thick and smooth. Beat in the eggs 1 at a time. Spread evenly over the pastry strips. Bake at 350 degrees for 1 hour.

To prepare the frosting, cream the butter and confectioners' sugar in a mixing bowl until light and fluffy, adding the milk as needed for the desired consistency. Mix in the almond flavoring. Spread over the pastry and sprinkle with almonds.

Serves four

OATMEAL SCONES

1 1/2 cups flour
1 1/4 cups uncooked quick-cooking oats
1/4 cup packed brown sugar
1 tablespoon baking powder
1/2 teaspoon salt
2/3 cup melted butter
1/2 cup milk
2 egg whites
1 teaspoon vanilla extract
1/2 cup raisins (optional)
1/3 cup chopped pecans (optional)
   Honey Butter with Strawberries (below)

Mix the flour, oats, brown sugar, baking powder and salt in a medium mixing bowl. Add the butter, milk, egg whites and vanilla and mix just until moistened. Stir in the raisins and pecans.

Shape into a ball and place on a lightly floured surface. Pat into a circle 3/4 inch thick. Cut into wedges or into the desired shapes with a cookie cutter. Place on a greased baking sheet. Bake at 425 degrees for 12 to 15 minutes or until golden brown. Serve with Honey Butter with Strawberries.

Add 1/2 cup dried cranberries and a dash of cinnamon for the holidays and cut into Christmas tree shapes.

Makes eight to twelve

HONEY BUTTER *with Strawberries makes the perfect accompaniment to warm scones, biscuits, and muffins. Purée 1 pint of strawberries in a food processor and strain to remove the seeds. Combine with 3 tablespoons honey, 1 teaspoon sugar, and 1 teaspoon fresh lime juice in a saucepan. Bring to a boil and cook for 3 minutes or until thickened. Cool to room temperature and combine with 3/4 cup softened unsalted butter. Let stand, covered, for 1 hour before serving. You may substitute 1 tablespoon orange juice and the grated zest of 1 orange or 1 pint of raspberries for the strawberries if preferred.*

BLUEBERRY OATMEAL MUFFINS

1/2 cup uncooked rolled oats
1/2 cup orange juice
1 or 2 eggs, lightly beaten
1/2 cup vegetable oil
11/2 cups flour
2 teaspoons baking powder
1/4 teaspoon baking soda
1/2 cup sugar
1/2 teaspoon salt
11/2 cups blueberries
1/4 cup sugar
1 tablespoon cinnamon

Mix the oats with the orange juice in a mixing bowl. Beat the eggs with the vegetable oil in a bowl and add to the oats mixture; mix well. Combine the flour, baking powder, baking soda, 1/2 cup sugar and salt in a medium bowl. Add to the oats mixture and mix just until moistened. Fold in the blueberries.

Grease the bottoms only of muffin cups. Spoon the batter into the muffin cups. Sprinkle with a mixture of 1/4 cup sugar and cinnamon. Bake at 400 degrees for 30 minutes.

You may also bake the batter in miniature muffin cups; reduce the baking time to 20 minutes. When using dark-colored or nonstick muffin pans, reduce the oven temperature to 375 degrees to prevent overbrowning of the muffin bottoms.
Makes twelve

ORANGE BLOSSOM MUFFINS

1 egg, lightly beaten
1/4 cup sugar
1/2 cup orange juice
2 tablespoons vegetable oil or melted shortening
2 cups baking mix
1/2 cup orange marmalade
1/2 teaspoon vanilla extract (optional)
1/2 cup chopped pecans
1/4 cup sugar
11/2 tablespoons flour
1/2 teaspoon cinnamon
1/4 teaspoon nutmeg
1 tablespoon butter or margarine

Combine the egg, 1/4 cup sugar, orange juice and vegetable oil in a mixing bowl and mix well. Add the baking mix and beat for 3 seconds. Stir in the marmalade, vanilla and pecans. Spoon into greased or paper-lined muffin cups, filling 2/3 full.

Mix 1/4 cup sugar, flour, cinnamon and nutmeg in a bowl. Cut in the butter until crumbly. Sprinkle over the muffins. Bake at 400 degrees for 20 to 25 minutes or until golden brown.
Makes twelve

COCONUT BANANA BREAD

1/2	cup shortening
1	cup sugar
2	eggs
1 1/2	cups flour
1	teaspoon baking soda
1/2	teaspoon salt
2	teaspoons vanilla extract
1 1/4	cups mashed bananas, about 3 bananas
3/4	cup sweetened flaked coconut

Cream the shortening and sugar in a mixing bowl until light and fluffy. Beat in the eggs. Add the flour, baking soda, salt and vanilla and mix well. Stir in the bananas and coconut. Spoon into a greased 5×9-inch loaf pan. Bake at 350 degrees for 1 hour or until a knife inserted in the center comes out clean.
Serves twelve

CRANBERRY BREAD

2	cups flour
1 1/2	teaspoons baking powder
1/2	teaspoon baking soda
1	cup sugar
1/2	teaspoon salt
	grated zest and juice of 1 orange
2	tablespoons melted shortening
	boiling water
1	egg
1	cup chopped fresh cranberries
3/4	cup chopped nuts (optional)

Mix the flour, baking powder, baking soda, sugar and salt in a large mixing bowl. Combine the orange zest and orange juice in a measuring cup. Add the melted shortening and enough boiling water to measure 3/4 cup and mix well. Add the egg and mix well.

Add the orange mixture to the dry ingredients and mix until smooth and thick. Stir in the cranberries and nuts. Spoon into a greased and floured 5×9-inch loaf pan. Bake at 325 degrees for 1 hour.
Serves twelve

ROSEMARY BREAD

3¹/3 cups bread flour
1¹/2 teaspoons salt
1   envelope dry yeast
1   tablespoon rosemary olive oil
1¹/4 cups lukewarm water
1   tablespoon chopped fresh rosemary
2   tablespoons cornmeal
1   egg white
1   tablespoon water

Mix the bread flour, salt and yeast in a large mixing bowl. Make a well in the center and add the olive oil, lukewarm water and rosemary. Mix with a wooden spoon to form a sticky dough. Knead on a lightly floured surface for 8 minutes or until smooth and elastic, dusting with additional flour if too sticky to handle. Place in a greased bowl, turning to coat the surface. Let rise, loosely covered with plastic wrap and a cloth, in a warm place for 1 hour or until doubled in bulk.

Place the dough on a lightly floured surface and punch down. Divide into 2 equal portions and shape into smooth balls. Cover loosely with waxed paper and let rest for 10 minutes.

Grease a baking sheet and sprinkle with the cornmeal. Shape each ball into a smooth oval loaf, pinching together any seams or creases on the bottoms of the loaves. Place on the prepared baking sheet and cut 3 diagonal slashes 1/4 inch deep in the top of each loaf. Cover loosely with waxed paper and let rise for 50 minutes or until doubled in bulk.

Beat the egg white lightly with the water in a small bowl. Brush over the loaves. Place in a 400-degree oven and place a shallow pan of boiling water on the rack below. Bake for 15 minutes. Brush again with the egg wash and bake for 10 minutes longer or until golden brown. Remove to a wire rack and let cool for 10 minutes to serve warm or cool to room temperature.
Makes two loaves

The photograph for this recipe is on page 25.

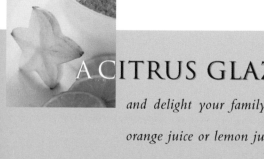

A CITRUS GLAZE *is a quick and easy way to add a burst of flavor to quick breads and delight your family and guests. Mix 1 cup confectioners' sugar with 1 to 2 tablespoons orange juice or lemon juice in a bowl. Drizzle the mixture onto cooled bread with a fork, using a sweeping motion. Slice the bread and serve with sliced fruit as a garnish. You can substitute milk for the fruit juice if preferred.*

ZUCCHINI BREAD

3	cups flour
1/2	teaspoon baking powder
2	teaspoons baking soda
1	teaspoon cinnamon
1/2	teaspoon ground cloves
1	teaspoon salt
3	cups shredded zucchini
1 2/3	cups sugar
2/3	cup vegetable oil
4	eggs
2	teaspoons vanilla extract
1/2	cup chopped pecans

Mix the flour, baking powder, baking soda, cinnamon, cloves and salt together. Combine the zucchini, sugar, vegetable oil, eggs and vanilla in a large mixing bowl and mix well. Add the dry ingredients and mix just until moistened. Fold in the pecans.

Grease the bottoms only of two 5×9-inch loaf pans. Spoon the batter into the prepared pans. Bake at 350 degrees for 1 hour and 10 minutes to 1 hour and 20 minutes or until a wooden pick inserted into the center comes out clean. Cool in the pans on wire racks for 10 minutes. Remove to the wire racks to cool completely.

Makes two loaves

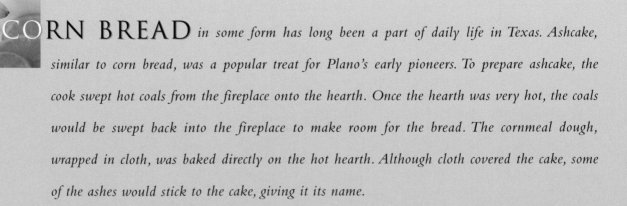

CORN BREAD *in some form has long been a part of daily life in Texas. Ashcake, similar to corn bread, was a popular treat for Plano's early pioneers. To prepare ashcake, the cook swept hot coals from the fireplace onto the hearth. Once the hearth was very hot, the coals would be swept back into the fireplace to make room for the bread. The cornmeal dough, wrapped in cloth, was baked directly on the hot hearth. Although cloth covered the cake, some of the ashes would stick to the cake, giving it its name.*

CORN BREAD

1¹/2	cups cornmeal
1	cup flour
¹/4	cup sugar
2¹/4	teaspoons baking powder
¹/2	teaspoon salt
1	medium fresh jalapeño pepper, seeded and finely chopped
1¹/4	cups milk
¹/4	cup vegetable oil
2	eggs, lightly beaten

Mix the cornmeal, flour, sugar, baking powder, salt and jalapeño pepper in a large bowl. Whisk the milk, vegetable oil and eggs in a small bowl until smooth. Add to the cornmeal mixture and mix well. Pour into a greased 8- or 9-inch square baking pan. Bake at 425 degrees for 20 minutes or until golden brown.
Serves six to eight

BLUE CORN MUFFINS

1	cup blue cornmeal
1	cup flour
1	tablespoon baking powder
³/4	cup (3 ounces) shredded Cheddar cheese with jalapeño pepper
¹/4	cup (¹/2 stick) butter, melted
2	tablespoons honey
2	eggs, beaten
1	cup milk
¹/2	cup chopped roasted green chiles or ¹/2 cup drained chopped canned green chiles
¹/4	cup (1 ounce) shredded Monterey Jack cheese

Mix the cornmeal, flour, baking powder and jalapeño cheese in a bowl. Combine the butter, honey, eggs, milk and green chiles in a small bowl and mix well. Add to the cornmeal mixture and mix just until moistened.

Spoon the batter in lightly greased 2-inch muffin cups, filling ³/4 full. Sprinkle with the Monterey Jack cheese. Bake at 350 degrees for 20 to 25 minutes or until golden brown.

You may substitute white or yellow cornmeal for the blue cornmeal in this recipe if preferred.
Makes twelve

The photographs for this recipe are on pages 14 and 15.

ABACUS' LOBSTER SCALLION SHOOTERS

This unique appetizer recipe was created by Kent Rathbun, renowned owner and chef of the Dallas restaurant Abacus. Since its inception in 1999, Abacus has been a hit, quickly becoming one of Dallas' most popular hot spots.

Red Coconut Curry Cream

6	garlic cloves, chopped
2	large shallots, chopped
2	ounces gingerroot, peeled and chopped
2	stalks lemon grass, chopped
1/4	cup sesame oil
2	kaffir lime leaves
1/2	cup rice vinegar
1/2	cup mirin
2	tablespoons red curry paste
2	(8-ounce) cans coconut milk
1	ounce cornstarch
1/2	bunch cilantro, coarsely chopped
	juice of 2 limes

Dumplings

1/4	cup sesame oil
4	garlic cloves, minced
2	shallots, minced
1	stalk lemon grass, minced
2	ounces gingerroot, peeled, minced
1	pound lobster meat, finely chopped
1	bunch scallions, chopped
1/4	cup tamari sauce
2	tablespoons sambal chile sauce
2	tablespoons chopped fresh mint
2	tablespoons chopped fresh basil
32	dumpling wrappers
1	egg, beaten
3	cups peanut oil

To prepare the cream, sauté the garlic, shallots, gingerroot and lemon grass in the sesame oil in a small saucepan until translucent but not brown. Add the kaffir lime leaves, rice vinegar, mirin and curry paste.

Cook until the liquid is reduced by half. Blend the coconut milk with the cornstarch in a bowl. Add to the saucepan and cook until thickened to the desired consistency, stirring constantly. Stir in the cilantro and lime juice. Strain through a fine strainer and reserve.

To prepare the dumplings, heat the sesame oil in a medium sauté pan. Add the garlic, shallots, lemon grass and gingerroot and sauté until light brown. Remove to a mixing bowl and fold in the lobster meat, scallions, tamari sauce, chile sauce, mint and basil.

Arrange the dumpling wrappers on a work surface and brush with the beaten egg. Place a small amount of the lobster mixture on each wrapper and fold the edges up to enclose the filling; press the edges to seal.

Preheat the peanut oil to 350 degrees in a deep fryer. Add the dumplings in batches and deep-fry until golden brown. Drain on paper towels. Serve with the curry cream.
Serves eight

PATRIZIO'S BRUSCHETTA

Whether you're in the mood for Belinis at the bar or Italian food al fresco, Patrizio's has it covered. Known for its bustling bar, pretty patio, and elegant interior, Patrizio's is a favorite "see and be seen" spot for North Texans.

1	loaf Italian or French bread
2	garlic cloves, chopped
1/2	cup olive oil
1/2	cup (1 stick) butter
3	tomatoes, chopped
6	garlic cloves, chopped
1/2	cup chopped fresh basil
	salt and pepper to taste
1/2	cup (2 ounces) grated Parmesan cheese

Slice the bread diagonally into 1-inch slices. Sauté 2 garlic cloves in 1 tablespoon of the olive oil in a small skillet. Add the butter and heat until the butter melts. Spread on the bread slices and place on a broiler pan.

Combine the tomatoes, 6 chopped garlic cloves, basil and the remaining olive oil in a bowl and mix well. Season with salt and pepper.

Broil the bread slices for 4 minutes or until light brown, watching closely. Remove from the broiler and adjust the oven to 400 degrees. Top the bread slices with the tomato mixture and sprinkle with the Parmesan cheese. Bake for 5 minutes and serve hot.

Serves six to eight

BLUE CHEESE CRISPS

2   cups (8 ounces) crumbled blue cheese
1/2   cup (1 stick) butter, softened
1 1/3 cups flour
1/3   cup poppy seeds
1/4   teaspoon ground red pepper

Combine the blue cheese and butter in a mixing bowl and beat at medium speed until fluffy. Add the flour, poppy seeds and red pepper and beat to form a smooth dough. Divide the dough into 2 portions and shape each portion into a 9-inch log. Chill, covered, for 2 hours.

Cut each log into 1/4-inch slices and arrange on an ungreased baking sheet. Bake at 350 degrees for 13 to 15 minutes or until golden brown. Remove to wire racks to cool completely.

Makes six dozen

ITALIAN CHEESE CRISPS

1 1/2 cups (6 ounces) grated fresh Parmesan cheese
1   tablespoon cornmeal
1/2   cup finely chopped pistachios
1/4   teaspoon garlic powder
1/8   teaspoon oregano
1/8   teaspoon ground red pepper
1/4   teaspoon black pepper

Combine the Parmesan cheese, cornmeal, pistachios, garlic powder, oregano, red pepper and black pepper in a bowl and mix well. Line 4 baking sheets with foil and spray with nonstick cooking spray. Spoon the cheese mixture into 2- to 3-inch mounds on the baking sheets, placing 8 mounds on each baking sheet. Bake at 350 degrees for 10 minutes or until light brown. Remove to a wire rack with a metal spatula to cool.

Makes thirty-two crisps

TEXAS WINE RECOMMENDATION: LA BODEGA WINERY COUNTRY BLUSH

A GATHERING *of friends is always a welcome distraction. Plan your next get-together by asking each friend to bring an appetizer. The party will become a wonderful exchange of new recipes and serving ideas. Many such gatherings were held while lovingly developing this cookbook and many ideas were exchanged. After all, sharing with family and friends is the best part of any meal.*

TOASTED CRAB MEAT TRIANGLES

1   loaf thin-sliced sandwich bread
8   ounces fresh crab meat
1/2 cup (2 ounces) shredded Monterey Jack cheese
1/2 cup (2 ounces) shredded Cheddar cheese
1/2 cup mayonnaise
1   (6-ounce) can water chestnuts, drained and chopped
4   green onion bulbs, chopped
1   teaspoon lemon juice
1/4 teaspoon curry powder

Cut the crusts from the bread slices and cut the slices into halves to form triangles. Combine the crab meat, Monterey Jack cheese, Cheddar cheese, mayonnaise, water chestnuts, green onions, lemon juice and curry powder in a bowl and mix well. Spread 1 tablespoon of the mixture onto each bread triangle. Place on a baking sheet and bake at 400 degrees for 10 to 12 minutes or until bubbly. Serve hot.

This appetizer was tested with Pepperidge Farms thin-sliced bread.

Serves twenty

MINIATURE BEEF TENDERLOINS WITH HORSERADISH SAUCE

2   pounds beef tenderloin
1   tablespoon olive oil
2   tablespoons crushed pepper
    sea salt to taste
1   tablespoon olive oil
1   cup prepared horseradish sauce
1   tablespoon chopped fresh thyme
    salt and pepper to taste
48 (1/4-inch) crostini
    sprigs of thyme

Cut the beef tenderloin lengthwise into 4 equal pieces. Brush with 1 tablespoon olive oil and rub 1/2 tablespoon of the crushed pepper into each piece. Season with the sea salt. Heat 1 tablespoon olive oil in a large skillet over high heat. Add the beef and sear for 3 to 4 minutes or until the outside is brown and the center is rare, turning to sear evenly. Remove from the heat and cool.

Combine the horseradish sauce and chopped thyme in a serving bowl. Season with salt and pepper. Cut the beef into 1/4-inch slices and place 1 on each crostini; top with the horseradish mixture and garnish each with a small sprig of thyme.

Makes forty-eight

TEXAS WINE RECOMMENDATION: BECKER VINEYARDS CABERNET SAUVIGNON

ONION TARTS

6	to 8 ounces chopped onions
1	tablespoon butter
12	ounces cream cheese, softened
1	cup (4 ounces) grated Parmesan cheese
1/4	cup mayonnaise
36	frozen phyllo cups
	green onions and/or paprika

Sauté the onions in the butter in a large skillet until translucent. Combine with the cream cheese, Parmesan cheese and mayonnaise in a bowl and mix well. Spoon into the phyllo cups and arrange on a baking sheet. Bake at 425 degrees for 6 to 8 minutes or until set. Garnish with green onions and/or paprika. You may also add salmon to the filling if desired.
Makes thirty-six

TEXAS WINE RECOMMENDATION: KIEPERSOL ESTATES MERLOT

STUFFED MUSHROOMS

1	pound fresh mushrooms
1/3	cup (1 1/3 ounces) finely chopped mozzarella cheese
1/2	cup (2 ounces) grated Parmesan cheese
3	green onions, chopped
8	slices bacon, crisp-fried and crumbled
1/4	cup (1/2 stick) butter or margarine, melted
3	tablespoons fine dry bread crumbs
1	garlic clove, minced

Remove and finely chop the mushroom stems, reserving the mushroom caps. Combine the chopped stems with the mozzarella cheese, Parmesan cheese, green onions, bacon, butter, bread crumbs and garlic in a bowl and mix well. Spoon into the reserved mushroom caps and arrange on a baking sheet. Bake at 325 degrees for 15 minutes.
Serves twelve

TEXAS WINE RECOMMENDATION: SPICEWOOD VINEYARDS MERLOT

AN **EXCELLENT WAY** *to keep mushroom caps from sliding around on the serving plate is to put a dab of cream cheese under each mushroom. This is especially helpful when they are being transported to someone else's home or when they are being passed on a tray.*

Won Tons

1	pound ground pork
1	pound frozen baby shrimp, chopped
2	(5-ounce) cans sliced water chestnuts, drained and chopped
1	cup chopped celery
1	cup chopped green onions
2	eggs, beaten
3	to 4 tablespoons soy sauce
1	tablespoon flour
2	tablespoons water
100	to 115 won ton wrappers
1	gallon peanut oil

Plum Sauce

1	(12-ounce) jar plum jelly
1	(6-ounce) jar chutney
4	teaspoons sugar
5	teaspoons vinegar

To prepare the won tons, brown the ground pork, stirring until crumbly; drain. Combine with the shrimp, water chestnuts, celery, green onions, eggs and soy sauce in a bowl and mix well. Chill for 30 minutes. Blend the flour and water in a small bowl to form a paste.

Place about 3/4 teaspoon of the pork mixture in the center of each won ton wrapper. Brush the edges of the wrappers with the flour paste and fold over the filling to form triangles. Fold the side points toward the larger point and seal with the flour paste. Deep-fry in the peanut oil until golden brown.

To prepare the plum sauce, combine the plum jelly, chutney, sugar and vinegar in a saucepan and mix well. Cook until heated through, stirring frequently. Serve with the won tons.

You may freeze the prepared won tons and reheat at 400 degrees for 10 to 15 minutes or until heated through.

Makes one hundred to one hundred fifteen

SPICED COCO-NUTS

1/2	cup sweetened flaked coconut
1/4	cup sugar
2	teaspoons curry powder
1	teaspoon salt
1/8	teaspoon cayenne pepper, or to taste
1	egg white
1	pound pecans, mixed nuts or other nuts

Combine the coconut, sugar, curry powder, salt and cayenne pepper in a large bowl and mix well. Whisk the egg white in a bowl until foamy. Add the nuts and stir to coat well. Add to the coconut mixture and toss to coat evenly. Spread in a single layer in a large buttered shallow baking pan. Place on the center rack of an oven heated to 300 degrees. Roast for 15 minutes or until crisp. Cool in the pan on a wire rack. Store in an airtight container at room temperature for up to 2 weeks.
Makes four cups

ROASTED PECANS

1/4	cup (1/2 stick) margarine
1	tablespoon Worcestershire sauce
3	cups shelled pecans
	seasoned salt to taste

Melt the margarine in a shallow baking pan. Stir in the Worcestershire sauce and add the pecans, mixing to coat well. Roast at 275 degrees for 45 minutes or until crisp, stirring every 15 minutes to avoid scorching. Remove to paper towels to drain and sprinkle with seasoned salt. Let stand until cool and store in an airtight container.
Makes three cups

TEXAS CAVIAR

2	(16-ounce) cans black-eyed peas, drained
1	(16-ounce) can yellow hominy, drained
1	cup chopped green bell pepper
1	cup chopped white onion
1	cup chopped tomato
1	cup chopped green onions
1/4	cup chopped jalapeño pepper
1/2	cup chopped cilantro
1	(16-ounce) jar picante sauce
1	tablespoon sugar
2	tablespoons cumin
1	teaspoon salt
2	teaspoons pepper

Combine the black-eyed peas, hominy, green pepper, onion, tomato, green onions, jalapeño pepper and cilantro in a medium bowl and mix well. Stir in the picante sauce, sugar, cumin, salt and pepper. Chill, covered, for 8 hours or longer. Serve with chips.
Serves fifteen

ROASTED CORN GUACAMOLE

6	tablespoons corn oil
2	cups frozen corn kernels, thawed
6	avocados, chopped
4	tomatoes, chopped
1/4	cup minced red onion
1/2	cup chopped cilantro
1/4	cup lime juice
2	teaspoons minced jalapeño pepper
2	teaspoons minced garlic
2	teaspoons apple cider vinegar
1/4	teaspoon cumin
1	tablespoon kosher salt

Spread 2 tablespoons of the corn oil on a baking sheet and add the corn. Roast at 450 degrees for 8 minutes. Transfer to a mixing bowl. Add the remaining 4 tablespoons corn oil, avocados, tomatoes, onion, cilantro, lime juice, jalapeño pepper, garlic, vinegar, cumin and kosher salt to the corn in the order listed and mix well. Chill until serving time. Serve with round tortilla chips.
Serves ten to twelve

The photograph for this recipe is on page 55.

CHICKEN ENCHILADA DIP

1/2	cup chopped onion
2	tablespoons butter
3	chicken breasts, cooked and chopped
1 1/2	cups (12 ounces) sour cream
3/4	cup (3 ounces) chopped processed cheese
3	tablespoons picante sauce
2	jalapeño peppers, seeded and chopped
3/4	cup crushed tortilla chips
1/2	cup (2 ounces) shredded Cheddar cheese

Sauté the onion in the butter in a saucepan. Add the chicken and sauté until heated. Stir in the sour cream, processed cheese, picante sauce, jalapeño peppers and crushed tortilla chips. Simmer until heated through. Spoon into a quiche pan or 9×9-inch baking pan and sprinkle with the Cheddar cheese. Bake at 350 degrees for 10 to 15 minutes or until the mixture is bubbly and the Cheddar cheese melts. Serve with tortilla chips.

You may microwave the mixture for 4 to 5 minutes if preferred. Serve leftovers in a soft tortilla as an easy luncheon dish.

Serves ten to twelve

CRAB DIP

1	(6-ounce) can crab meat
8	ounces cream cheese, softened
2	tablespoons mayonnaise
2	dashes of lemon juice
1/4	onion, chopped
1/2	cup chopped fresh parsley
1	(2-ounce) package slivered almonds, toasted
	paprika to taste
	lemon wedges

Combine the crab meat with the cream cheese, mayonnaise, lemon juice and onion in a bowl and mix well. Spoon into a 6×6-inch baking dish. Bake at 350 degrees for 15 minutes. Top with the parsley and almonds. Garnish with paprika and lemon wedges. Serve hot with crackers.

Serves six to eight

HUMMUS

2	(16-ounce) cans chick-peas
1	small garlic clove, or to taste
1/4	cup light soy sauce
2	tablespoons lemon juice
2	tablespoons minced fresh parsley, or 1 tablespoon dried parsley
2	teaspoons cumin
1	teaspoon chili powder
1	teaspoon paprika
1	teaspoon white pepper

Drain 1 can of the chick-peas. Combine the drained chick-peas, the undrained chick-peas, garlic, soy sauce, lemon juice, parsley, cumin, chili powder, paprika and white pepper in a food processor or blender. Process until smooth. Spoon into a serving bowl and serve with Pita Chips (below) or whole wheat pita bread.

Serves twelve

PECOS DIP

16	ounces cream cheese, softened
1	cup hot salsa
1	(2¹/2-ounce) jar dried beef, finely chopped
1	cup finely chopped green onions with tops
1	teaspoon ground cumin
1/2	teaspoon oregano

Combine the cream cheese and salsa in a mixing bowl and mix well. Stir in the dried beef, green onions, cumin and oregano. Chill until serving time. Serve with tortilla chips.

You should not prepare this dip in a food processor.

Serves twelve

PITA CHIPS *are a delicious accompaniment to hummus. To prepare the chips, split two pita bread rounds into halves horizontally and cut each half into six wedges. Arrange the wedges in a single layer on a baking sheet. Brush lightly with olive oil or spray with nonstick cooking spray. Sprinkle with ¹/4 to ¹/2 teaspoon garlic salt. Bake at 400 degrees for 6 to 8 minutes or until crisp and light brown.*

GAZPACHO DIP

3	tablespoons olive oil
1 1/2	tablespoons cider vinegar
1	teaspoon garlic salt
1	teaspoon salt
1/4	teaspoon pepper
1	(4-ounce) can chopped black olives
1	(4-ounce) can chopped green chiles
4	or 5 green onions, chopped
2	or 3 tomatoes, chopped
2	or 3 avocados, chopped
	chopped cilantro to taste

Blend the olive oil and vinegar in a bowl. Add the garlic salt, salt and pepper and mix well. Stir in the undrained olives and green chiles. Add the green onions, tomatoes and avocados and mix well. Chill for several hours. Garnish with cilantro. Serve with tortilla chips.
Serves six to eight

TEXAS WINE RECOMMENDATION: CAP ROCK WINERY CABERNET ROYALE

MASA CALIENTE

1	(15-ounce) can corn, drained
2	(4-ounce) cans chopped green chiles
1	cup (4 ounces) shredded Monterey Jack cheese
1/2	cup chopped red bell pepper
2	tablespoons chopped jalapeño peppers
1	cup mayonnaise
1/2	cup (2 ounces) grated Parmesan cheese
2	tablespoons sliced black olives

Combine the corn, green chiles, Monterey Jack cheese, bell pepper and jalapeño peppers in a bowl and mix well. Stir in the mayonnaise and Parmesan cheese. Spoon into an ungreased 2-quart baking dish. Bake, covered, at 350 degrees for 30 minutes or until heated through. Sprinkle with the olives and serve with tortilla chips.

Light mayonnaise or low-fat mayonnaise is not recommended for this recipe.
Makes three cups

TEXAS WINE RECOMMENDATION: HAAK VINEYARDS BLANC DU BOIS

SPICY SPINACH AND ARTICHOKE DIP

8	ounces cream cheese, softened
2	cups (8 ounces) grated Parmesan cheese
3/4	cup mayonnaise
1	tablespoon minced garlic
2	teaspoons basil
1 1/2	teaspoons cayenne pepper
1	(6-ounce) jar marinated artichoke hearts, drained and chopped
2	(10-ounce) packages frozen chopped spinach, thawed
2	cups (8 ounces) shredded Cheddar cheese
2	cups (8 ounces) shredded Monterey Jack cheese

Combine the cream cheese, Parmesan cheese, mayonnaise, garlic, basil and cayenne pepper in a mixing bowl and mix until smooth. Add the artichoke hearts and mix well. Press the spinach to remove the excess moisture. Add to the cream cheese mixture with the Cheddar cheese and Monterey Jack cheese; mix well. Spoon into a 2-quart baking dish. Bake at 375 degrees for 40 minutes. Blot the surface with a paper towel and serve with tortilla chips. *Serves fifteen*

TEXAS WINE RECOMMENDATION: DRY COMAL CREEK VINEYARDS SAUVIGNON BLANC

CHOOSING A WINE *can sometimes be intimidating. Here are some simple guidelines to help you. Lighter fare tastes best with a delicate wine like Chardonnay that won't overpower the food. A fuller-bodied wine like a Merlot or a Cabernet Sauvignon won't get lost when served with heavier or spicy foods. Keep in mind that sweet foods can make your wine seem drier, so serve them with a slightly sweeter wine like a Reisling. Bitter and tannic foods are best paired with a fruity wine like Pinot Grigio. Finally, there is the question of temperature. White, rosé, and sparkling wines are best chilled but not icy cold enough to dull their flavors. Most red wines taste best slightly cooler than room temperature.*

TEXAS STAR SPINACH DIP

Spinach Dip Mix

1 (16-ounce) package frozen chopped spinach, thawed
1 1/2 tablespoons unsalted butter
3 tablespoons flour
2 cups half-and-half
1/2 cup (2 ounces) grated Parmesan cheese
1 tablespoon hot pepper sauce
1 1/2 teaspoons kosher salt

Dip

1 cup Spinach Dip Mix
1 cup (4 ounces) shredded Cheddar cheese
1 cup (4 ounces) shredded mozzarella cheese
1 cup (8 ounces) sour cream
1 cup finely chopped red onion
1 cup crumbled crisp-fried bacon
1 (16-ounce) jar salsa

To prepare the dip mix, drain the spinach, pressing to remove the excess moisture. Melt the butter in a large skillet and whisk in the flour. Cook until bubbly, whisking constantly. Add the half-and-half and cook until thickened, stirring constantly. Remove from the heat and stir in the Parmesan cheese, hot sauce and kosher salt. Let stand until cool. Stir in the spinach. Reserve 1 cup of the mixture for the dip. Store the remaining mix in the refrigerator or freezer for another use.

To prepare the dip, combine the reserved 1 cup dip mix with the Cheddar cheese and mozzarella cheese in a bowl and mix well. Spoon into a baking dish. Bake at 350 degrees for 10 minutes. Stir the mixture well and bake for 5 minutes longer or until light brown.

Spoon the sour cream, onion, bacon and salsa into bowls to accompany the dip. Serve with tortilla chips.

Serves six to eight

TEXAS WINE RECOMMENDATION: BRUSHY CREEK VINEYARDS AUTUMN SUNSET

BLACK BEAN SALSA

2   (16-ounce) cans black beans
1   (16-ounce) can corn
10 Roma tomatoes, chopped
2   bunches green onions, chopped
1   or 2 jalapeño peppers, chopped
1   bunch cilantro, leaves only, chopped
1/2 cup red wine vinegar
1/4 cup lime juice
1   tablespoon chili powder
1 1/2 teaspoons salt

Drain and rinse the black beans and corn. Combine with the tomatoes, green onions, jalapeño peppers, cilantro, wine vinegar, lime juice, chili powder and salt in a bowl and mix well. Chill for 30 minutes, stirring 2 or 3 times. Serve chilled or at room temperature with tortilla chips.
Serves twenty

FETA SALSA

1   cup (4 ounces) crumbled feta cheese
1/4 cup chopped Italian parsley
15 to 20 kalamata olives, chopped
2/3 (15-ounce) can diced tomatoes or tomatoes with roasted garlic, drained
2   green onions, chopped
2   tablespoons capers
1   tablespoon (heaping) dillweed
3   tablespoons olive oil
1/4 cup fresh lime juice
    freshly ground pepper to taste
1   baguette, sliced into 1/4-inch rounds

Combine the feta cheese, parsley, olives, tomatoes and green onions in a bowl. Add the capers, dillweed, olive oil, lime juice and pepper and mix well. Chill in the refrigerator. Serve with the baguette rounds.
Serves twelve

SESAME EGGPLANT SALSA

3	pounds eggplant
3	tablespoons light brown sugar
2	tablespoons soy sauce
1	tablespoon rice vinegar
2	teaspoons fresh lemon juice
1	tablespoon olive oil
3/4	cup minced green onions
2¹/2	tablespoons grated gingerroot
4	garlic cloves, chopped
1	teaspoon garlic chili sauce
2	large tomatoes, chopped, or 1 cup diced canned tomatoes
3/4	cup finely chopped cilantro
1¹/2	teaspoons sesame oil
	salt and pepper to taste
1	tablespoon minced green onions
1	tablespoon finely chopped cilantro

Cut the eggplant into halves lengthwise. Place cut side down on an oiled baking sheet. Bake at 425 degrees for 1 hour or until very tender. Scoop the pulp from the skins and place in a colander over a large bowl to drain for 30 minutes if necessary to remove excess liquid. Process in a food processor until nearly smooth.

Combine the brown sugar, soy sauce, rice vinegar and lemon juice in a bowl and mix well. Heat the olive oil in a skillet over medium-high heat. Add 3/4 cup green onions, gingerroot, garlic and chili sauce. Sauté for 1 minute. Stir in the brown sugar mixture and bring to a simmer, stirring constantly. Stir in the eggplant and cook until heated through.

Remove from the heat and stir in the tomatoes, 3/4 cup cilantro and sesame oil. Let stand until cool and season with salt and pepper. Spoon into a serving bowl and sprinkle with 1 tablespoon minced green onions and 1 tablespoon chopped cilantro. Serve with tortilla chips.
Serves twenty-four

WATERMELON SALSA

2	cups coarsely chopped watermelon
1	cup roasted corn kernels
1/2	cup chopped red onion
1	large jalapeño pepper, seeded and chopped
	juice of 1 lime

Combine the watermelon, corn, onion, jalapeño pepper and lime juice in a bowl and mix gently. Chill until serving time.

Serve with tortilla chips, over salads or with grilled chicken or fish.
Serves six

SWISS FONDUE

3	cups (12 ounces) shredded Swiss cheese, at room temperature
2	cups (8 ounces) shredded Gruyère cheese, at room temperature
3	tablespoons flour
1 1/2	cups dry white wine
2	tablespoons dry sherry
1/3	cup milk
1/8	teaspoon garlic powder
1/8	teaspoon ground nutmeg
1/8	teaspoon white pepper
1	loaf French bread, cut into 1-inch cubes

Mix the Swiss cheese, Gruyère cheese and flour in a bowl. Bring the white wine just to a boil in a saucepan over medium heat. Reduce the heat to low and add the cheese mixture gradually, stirring until the cheese is melted and the mixture is smooth. Bring just to a simmer and stir in the sherry, milk, garlic powder, nutmeg and white pepper. Spoon into a fondue pot. Provide fondue forks to dip the bread cubes into the fondue.

You may also serve the fonduc with bite-size fruits and vegetables.

Serves twelve

BAKED BRIE WITH BROWN SUGAR AND ALMONDS

1	(8-ounce) round Brie cheese
1/2	cup sliced almonds
1/4	cup packed light brown sugar

Cut off and discard the top rind of the cheese. Place the cheese cut side up in a heat-proof serving dish. Mix the almonds and brown sugar in a bowl and sprinkle over the top of the cheese. Bake at 400 degrees on the top oven rack for 12 minutes or until the brown sugar is bubbly and the cheese is hot and soft. Serve with baguette slices or crackers.

Serves eight to ten

THE HOT TEXAS SUN *brings on a thirst that can only be quenched by delving into a delicious Texas watermelon. At the peak of ripeness a watermelon should be firm, symmetrical, and heavy. Another sign of perfection is a creamy yellow spot on the underside of the melon indicating that it was sun-ripened. Watermelons are produced in almost every county in Texas and are harvested and sold throughout the world eleven months of the year.*

BAKED BRIE WITH PESTO AND TUSCANY TOAST

Pesto

1	cup chopped fresh basil
2	garlic cloves
3	tablespoons pine nuts
1/4	cup olive oil

Baked Brie and Tuscany Toast

2	baguettes
	olive oil
1	ounce sun-dried tomatoes, chopped
1/2	cup (2 ounces) grated Parmesan cheese
1	(8-ounce) round Brie cheese

To prepare the pesto, combine the basil, garlic, pine nuts and olive oil in a food processor and process into a thick paste.

To prepare the Brie and toast, cut the baguettes into 1/4-inch slices. Brush with olive oil and arrange on a baking sheet. Toast in a 400-degree oven just until slightly dried; do not brown. Reserve 1/4 cup of the pesto and spread the remaining pesto on the toast. Top with the sun-dried tomatoes and Parmesan cheese. Bake at 400 degrees for 8 minutes or until golden brown and crisp.

Brush the remaining pesto on the top of the Brie cheese and place on a baking sheet. Bake at 400 degrees for 8 minutes or until soft. Place on a serving plate and arrange the toast around the cheese.
Serves eight

The photographs for this recipe are on pages 20 and 21.

CRANBERRY CHUTNEY *is a wonderfully delicious topping for baked Brie. Bring 2/3 cup sugar and 2/3 cup water to a boil in a saucepan and cook until the sugar dissolves. Add 1/2 cup cranberries, 4 teaspoons vinegar, 1/4 cup walnuts, 2 teaspoons brown sugar, and 1/4 teaspoon ground ginger. Cook for 7 to 10 minutes or until thickened, stirring frequently. Cut the top rind from the Brie cheese and place it in a baking dish. Spread the cranberry mixture over the top and bake at 350 degrees for 10 to 15 minutes or until the topping is bubbly and the cheese is soft.*

PESTO CREAM CHEESE WITH TOMATO BASIL RELISH

4   Roma tomatoes, seeded, drained and chopped
1/4 cup chopped fresh basil
1/3 cup (1 1/3 ounces) finely grated Parmesan cheese
2   tablespoons chopped garlic
2   tablespoons olive oil
     salt and pepper to taste
4   to 6 ounces fresh or commercially prepared pesto
12 ounces cream cheese, softened
     fresh basil sprigs
1   baguette, sliced 1/4 inch thick

Combine the tomatoes, chopped basil, Parmesan cheese, garlic, olive oil, salt and pepper in a bowl and mix well. Spoon into a 9-inch baking dish. Bake at 350 degrees for 30 minutes or until the tomatoes are tender and the mixture is heated through. Stir to mix well and cool slightly.

Mix the prepared pesto with the cream cheese in a bowl. Mound in a serving dish. Top with the baked tomato mixture and garnish with fresh basil. Serve with the sliced baguette.
Serves sixteen

TEXAS WINE RECOMMENDATION: PLEASANT HILL WINERY SAUVIGNON BLANC

HERBED CHÈVRE SPREAD WITH CUCUMBER AND LEMON HONEY DRESSING

Herbed Chèvre Spread

1 1/2 cups (6 ounces) crumbled goat cheese
8   ounces nonfat cream cheese
1/4 cup plain nonfat yogurt
2   garlic cloves, crushed
1   tablespoon chopped chives
1   teaspoon chopped fresh thyme leaves, or 1/2 teaspoon dried thyme
     salt and freshly ground pepper to taste

Cucumber and Lemon Honey Dressing

1   tablespoon lemon juice
1   tablespoon honey
1   medium seedless cucumber, thinly sliced
     freshly ground pepper to taste

To prepare the spread, combine the goat cheese, cream cheese, yogurt and garlic in a food processor and process until smooth. Remove to a serving bowl and fold in the chives and thyme; do not overmix. Season with salt and pepper. Chill for 4 hours or until slightly firm.

To prepare the cucumber and dressing, combine the lemon juice and honey in a bowl and mix well. Place the cheese mixture in the center of a serving plate and drizzle with the dressing. Arrange the cucumber slices around the cheese and sprinkle with pepper.
Serves ten to twelve

TEXAS WINE RECOMMENDATION: TEXAS HILLS PINOT GRIGIO

SWEET AND SPICY CHEESE SPREAD

8	ounces cream cheese, softened
1	tablespoon grated onion
1	garlic clove, minced
1/4	cup (1/2 stick) butter
1/4	cup packed dark brown sugar
1	teaspoon Worcestershire sauce
1/4	teaspoon Tabasco sauce
1	cup pecans, toasted and chopped

Combine the cream cheese, onion and garlic in a bowl and mix well. Shape into 1 disk 1 inch thick and place on a serving plate. Chill in the refrigerator.

Melt the butter in a saucepan. Add the brown sugar, Worcestershire sauce and Tabasco sauce and mix well. Stir in the pecans. Spread over the cream cheese mixture. Chill for several hours. Serve at room temperature with crackers.

Serves eight to ten

RASPBERRY CHEESE TORTE

6	cups (11/2 pounds) shredded sharp Cheddar cheese
1/4	onion, finely minced
3/4	cup chopped pecans
1/2	cup mayonnaise
1/4	to 1/2 teaspoon Tabasco sauce
1/4	teaspoon cayenne pepper
1	cup raspberry preserves

Combine the Cheddar cheese, onion, pecans, mayonnaise, Tabasco sauce and cayenne pepper in a food processor and process until smooth. Press the mixture firmly into a springform pan lined with plastic wrap. Chill for 4 hours or longer. Unmold the torte onto a serving plate and remove the plastic wrap. Spread the preserves on the top and serve with crackers.

Serves twenty

TOMATO PESTO TORTE

8	ounces each cream cheese and chèvre, softened
1/2	cup fresh or commercially prepared pesto
1	(12-ounce) jar sun-dried tomatoes, drained and chopped
1/2	cup crushed walnuts
	grated Parmesan cheese

Combine the cream cheese and chèvre in a bowl and mix well. Spread in a springform pan lined with plastic wrap. Layer the pesto, sun-dried tomatoes and walnuts over the cheese mixture in the order listed. Chill in the refrigerator. Unmold the torte onto a serving plate and remove the plastic wrap. Top with Parmesan cheese and serve with crackers.
Serves sixteen

TEXAS WINE RECOMMENDATION: LONE OAK VINEYARDS MERLOT

CILANTRO MOUSSE

2	envelopes unflavored gelatin
1/2	cup water
1	tablespoon chicken bouillon granules
6	serrano peppers
1	bunch cilantro
1	small yellow onion
8	ounces cream cheese, softened
1	cup mayonnaise
1/2	cup milk

Sprinkle the gelatin over the water in a saucepan and let stand until softened. Bring to a boil and add the chicken bouillon, stirring to dissolve the bouillon and gelatin.

Discard the seeds from the peppers. Combine the peppers with the cilantro and onion in a food processor and pulse until finely chopped. Add the cream cheese and mayonnaise and pulse to mix well. Drizzle in the milk and then the bouillon mixture, processing constantly until smooth. Spoon the mixture into a greased mold. Chill until firm and set. Unmold onto a serving plate and serve with crackers.
Serves ten to twelve

TO **UNMOLD GELATIN,** *loosen the edges with a knife tip; then place the serving plate over the mold and invert. If it does not release, you can heat the mold with a hair dryer or place the mold in a bowl of hot water for a few seconds. To better position the congealed mixture after it has been unmolded, first wet the plate to prevent sticking. To dissolve gelatin smoothly, first soften it for five minutes in at least 1/4 cup of the liquid called for in the recipe and then heat it over low heat until it dissolves completely, stirring constantly.*

FROZEN DAIQUIRIS

2	(6-ounce) cans frozen limeade concentrate, thawed
1	(6-ounce) can pink lemonade concentrate, thawed
1	(6-ounce) can frozen orange juice concentrate, thawed
1	(8-ounce) bottle of maraschino cherries, drained
6	cups water
26	ounces rum

Combine the limeade concentrate, lemonade concentrate, orange juice concentrate, cherries, water and rum in a 1-gallon freezer container and mix well. Freeze for 1 or 2 days, stirring 3 or more times each day.
Serves ten

MIMI'S MANGO MARGARITAS

1	(12-ounce) jar mangoes
1	(6-ounce) can frozen limeade concentrate, thawed
1	cup gold tequila
1/4	cup Triple Sec
1/4	cup Grand Marnier
1	lime
	sugar

Process the undrained mangoes in a blender until smooth. Add the limeade concentrate, tequila, Triple Sec and Grand Marnier and process until well mixed. Remove and reserve half the mixture. Fill the blender container with ice and add half the margarita mixture; process until smooth. Repeat the process with the remaining margarita mixture.

Rub the rims of large glasses with juice from the lime and coat with sugar. Pour the margaritas into the prepared glasses and garnish with lime slices.

Jars of mangoes can usually be found in the refrigerated produce section of the market.
Serves four

The photograph for this recipe is on page 55.

RED ROOSTERS

4   cups (1 quart) cranberry juice
6   cups (1 1/2 quarts) fresh orange juice
4   cups (1 quart) vodka
     cranberries and orange slices

Combine the cranberry juice, orange juice and vodka in a large freezer container and freeze until slushy. Let stand at room temperature for a short time before serving. Serve as it is or process in a blender if preferred. Garnish the servings with cranberries and orange slices.
Serves twenty-four

YELLOW BIRD

1/4   cup sugar
1/4   cup water
1   cup orange juice
1/2   cup lemon juice
1/2   cup light rum
1/4   cup apricot brandy
1/4   cup banana liqueur

Mix the sugar and water in a saucepan and bring to a boil. Cook until the sugar dissolves completely, stirring constantly. Let stand until cool.

Combine the sugar syrup with the orange juice, lemon juice, rum, apricot brandy and banana liqueur in a pitcher and mix well.
Serves four

TEXAS SUNSETS *inspire us to be bold with our entertaining. Make your next cocktail party a sunset occasion. Serve beverages and appetizers outside and enjoy the beautiful sun setting on the horizon. Set out blankets and chairs and enjoy! You and your guests will still be outside when the stars come out.*

CLASSIC PUNCH

1   (32-ounce) can pineapple juice
1   (12-ounce) can frozen orange juice concentrate, thawed
1   (12-ounce) can frozen lemonade concentrate, thawed
4   cups (1 quart) light rum
2   liters lemon-lime soda

Combine the pineapple juice, orange juice concentrate, lemonade concentrate and rum in a large freezer container and mix well. Freeze for 8 hours or longer. Combine with the lemon-lime soda in a punch bowl at serving time and mix gently.
Serves twenty-four

SHOWER PUNCH

Ice Ring

     strawberries
4   cups (1 quart) ginger ale

Punch

1   (12-ounce) can frozen lemonade concentrate, thawed
1   (12-ounce) can frozen orange juice concentrate, thawed
1   (32-ounce) can pineapple juice
6   cups ginger ale
1   teaspoon vanilla extract
1/2   teaspoon almond extract
1   quart pineapple sherbet

To prepare the ice ring, arrange strawberries in a ring mold and add 1 cup of the ginger ale. Freeze for several hours. Add the remaining 3 cups ginger ale and freeze for 8 hours or longer.

To prepare the punch, combine the lemonade concentrate, orange juice concentrate, pineapple juice, ginger ale and flavorings in a large punch bowl and mix gently. Scoop the sherbet into the punch.

Place the ice ring mold in a bowl of warm water just long enough to loosen. Remove the ring from the mold and float in the punch.
Serves twenty-five

TROPICAL BANANA PUNCH

3   cups sugar
3   cups unsweetened pineapple juice
1   (6-ounce) can frozen orange juice concentrate, thawed
1   (6-ounce) can water
     juice of 2 large lemons
4   bananas, mashed
8   cups (64 ounces) lemon-lime soda

   Dissolve the sugar in the pineapple juice in a large freezer container. Add the orange juice concentrate, water, lemon juice and bananas and mix well. Freeze for 8 hours or longer. Let stand at room temperature for 30 minutes. Combine with the lemon-lime soda in a punch bowl at serving time and mix gently.
Serves ten to twelve

SOUTHERN LEMONADE

4   lemons
4   oranges
4   limes
1 1/2 to 2 cups sugar
1   gallon water

   Squeeze the juice from the lemons, oranges and limes. Combine the juices in a 1-gallon container. Add the sugar and water and mix to dissolve the sugar completely.
Serves eight

The photograph for this recipe is on page 19.

DRESS UP ICE CUBES *for a special occasion. Start freezing ice cubes several days in advance and remove to plastic bags to store until you have enough. You can add raspberries to cubes made of water or freeze sweetened fruit purée in candy molds to create interesting shapes and provide a delicious addition to glasses, pitchers, or a punch bowl.*

SUMMERTIME TEA

16   cups (1 gallon) water
5   (1-quart) tea bags
3/4   cup sugar
1   (12-ounce) can frozen lemonade concentrate, thawed
2   teaspoons almond extract
8   lemon slices
      mint sprigs

Bring the water to a boil in a large saucepan and remove from the heat. Add the tea bags and steep until of the desired strength. Remove the tea bags and combine the tea with the sugar in a large container, stirring to dissolve the sugar completely. Add the lemonade concentrate and almond extract and mix well. Pour over ice in tall glasses and garnish with lemon slices and mint sprigs.
Serves eight

HOT BUTTERED RUM

1/2   cup (1 stick) butter
1   (1-pound) package brown sugar
1/4   teaspoon ground cloves
1/2   to 1 teaspoon cinnamon
1/2   teaspoon allspice
41/2 cups rum, or 3 tablespoons for each serving

Melt the butter in a saucepan and add the brown sugar, cloves, cinnamon and allspice, stirring to dissolve the brown sugar completely. Combine 1 tablespoon of the mixture with 3 tablespoons rum in a mug for each serving and fill the mug with hot water.

You may store the brown sugar mixture in an airtight container in the refrigerator until needed. Do not substitute margarine for the butter in this recipe.
Serves twenty-four

SPICED COFFEE

2¹/₂   cups instant coffee granules
2¹/₂   cups powdered nondairy coffee creamer
1¹/₂   cups hot cocoa mix
1¹/₂   cups sugar
1   teaspoon cinnamon
¹/₂   teaspoon nutmeg
¹/₄   teaspoon allspice
¹/₄   teaspoon ground cloves

Mix the coffee granules, coffee creamer and cocoa mix in a blender. Combine with the sugar, cinnamon, nutmeg, allspice and cloves in an airtight container and mix well. Place 2 tablespoons of the mixture in a mug for each serving and fill the mug with hot water. Top the servings with whipped cream if desired.
Serves sixty-four

GOLDEN WASSAIL

4   cups unsweetened pineapple juice
1   (12-ounce) can apricot nectar
4   cups apple cider
1   cup orange juice
1   (6-inch) cinnamon stick, crumbled
1   teaspoon whole cloves
¹/₄   teaspoon whole cardamom seeds
¹/₄   teaspoon salt

Combine the pineapple juice, apricot nectar, apple cider and orange juice in an 18- to 20-cup percolator. Combine the cinnamon, cloves, cardamom seeds and salt in the basket. Perk the mixture through a regular cycle and serve hot from the percolator.
Serves twenty

THE MANSION ON TURTLE CREEK TORTILLA SOUP

Dean Fearing of The Mansion on Turtle Creek in Dallas contributed this delectable tortilla soup recipe. He has received countless culinary awards, and is regarded as the Father of Southwestern Cuisine.

5	dried New Mexican chiles
3	tablespoons corn oil
4	corn tortillas, cut into long strips
8	garlic cloves, chopped
2	cups fresh onion purée
4	cups fresh tomato purée
2	jalapeño peppers, chopped
1	tablespoon chopped epazote, or 2 tablespoons chopped fresh cilantro
1	tablespoon ground cumin
1	teaspoon ground coriander
1	large bay leaf
1 1/2	quarts chicken stock
	lemon juice to taste
	salt and cayenne pepper to taste
1	boneless skinless chicken breast, cooked and cut into thin strips
1	large avocado, chopped
1 1/2	cups (6 ounces) shredded Cheddar cheese
4	corn tortillas, cut into thin strips and crisp-fried

Grasp 1 chile pepper at a time with kitchen tongs and hold directly over an open flame for 30 to 45 seconds or until lightly roasted on all sides, taking care not to blacken or burn. Cool and chop the chiles, discarding the seeds and stems.

Heat the corn oil in a large saucepan over medium heat. Add the tortilla strips and garlic and sauté for 4 to 5 minutes or until the tortilla strips are crisp and the garlic is golden brown. Add the onion purée and cook for 5 minutes or until reduced by half, stirring occasionally.

Add the tomato purée, roasted chiles, jalapeño peppers, epazote, cumin, coriander, bay leaf and chicken stock. Bring to a boil and reduce the heat. Simmer for 40 minutes, skimming the surface if necessary. Discard the bay leaf and process the soup in a food mill or blender until smooth, adding additional chicken stock if needed. Season with lemon juice, salt and cayenne pepper.

Ladle the soup into soup bowls and top each serving with chicken, avocado, Cheddar cheese and crisp tortilla strips. Serve immediately. You may also roast the chiles in a 400-degree oven if preferred.

Serves four

NEIMAN MARCUS CRUNCHY THAI SALAD

After a morning of shopping at Neiman Marcus, visitors find a respite from high fashion at Mariposa's or the Zodiac Room to enjoy a delectable lunch.

Thai Dressing

1/4	cup fresh lime juice
3	tablespoons olive oil
1	tablespoon sesame oil
1	tablespoon soy sauce
1	large pinch of brown sugar
1/2	garlic clove, minced
1	red chile pepper, seeded and thinly sliced
1	tablespoon finely chopped gingerroot
1	large handful of finely chopped cilantro and basil

Crunchy Thai Salad

1	package cellophane noodles
3	cups baby spinach
1	bunch arugula
1	head Napa cabbage, thinly sliced
1	red bell pepper, thinly sliced
1	green bell pepper, thinly sliced
1	red chile pepper, seeded and thinly sliced
1	European cucumber, thinly sliced and seeded
1	pound sugar snap peas
1	pound bean sprouts
2	(8-ounce) boneless skinless chicken breasts, or 16 ounces chicken tenderloins
1	cup lightly toasted cashews
1	tablespoon finely chopped fresh mint
1	tablespoon finely chopped fresh basil
1	tablespoon finely chopped cilantro

To prepare the dressing, combine the lime juice, olive oil, sesame oil and soy sauce in a bowl and mix well. Add the brown sugar, garlic, chile pepper, gingerroot and mixture of cilantro and basil and mix well.

To prepare the salad, cook the noodles using the package directions. Combine the spinach, arugula and Napa cabbage in a salad bowl and toss to mix. Spoon onto 4 serving plates. Sprinkle the bell peppers, chile pepper, cucumber and snap peas over the greens. Twirl a small amount of the noodles at a time around a fork and place over the salads. Top with the bean sprouts.

Cut the chicken into strips and grill for 3 to 4 minutes on each side or until cooked through. Arrange on the salads. Sprinkle with the cashews and chopped mint, basil and cilantro. Drizzle with the dressing.
Serves four

CHEFS' RECIPES

BASIL AND CHEESE SALAD WITH PECANS

10	ounces salad greens
3	cups (12 ounces) shredded mozzarella cheese
1/2	cup (2 ounces) grated Parmesan cheese
1	tablespoon chopped fresh basil, or 1/2 teaspoon dried basil
4	large tomatoes, chopped
1	cup Texas pecans, finely chopped
1/4	cup basil olive oil
1	tablespoon white wine vinegar

Combine the salad greens with the mozzarella cheese, Parmesan cheese, basil, tomatoes and pecans in a bowl. Add the olive oil and vinegar and toss to coat well.
Serves eight

CRUNCHY COLESLAW

Ramen Dressing

1	cup vegetable oil
1/2	cup vinegar
2	tablespoons soy sauce
1	cup sugar
	seasoning packet from 1 package ramen noodles

Coleslaw

1/2	cup (1 stick) margarine
2	(3-ounce) packages ramen noodles, seasoning packets removed
1/4	cup sesame seeds
1/2	cup slivered almonds
1	head cabbage, sliced
5	green onions, chopped

To prepare the dressing, combine the vegetable oil, vinegar, soy sauce, sugar and seasoning packet from the ramen noodles in a jar and shake to blend well.

To prepare the salad, heat the margarine in a skillet. Break the ramen noodles into small pieces and add to the skillet. Add the sesame seeds and almonds and sauté until crisp and brown. Drain on paper towels. Combine the cabbage, green onions, noodle mixture and dressing in a salad bowl and toss to coat well. Serve immediately.

You may prepare the noodle mixture in advance and store in an airtight container. Chill the cabbage and green onion mixture until time to add the noodle mixture and dressing.
Serves ten

CREAMY COLESLAW

Coleslaw

1 1/2 pounds cabbage, finely shredded
1 small carrot, scraped and chopped
1/2 cup chopped green bell pepper
1/2 cup chopped celery
1/4 cup chopped green onions

Coleslaw Dressing

1/2 cup mayonnaise
1/2 cup (4 ounces) sour cream
2 tablespoons sugar
2 tablespoons vinegar
1 tablespoon prepared mustard
1/2 teaspoon paprika
1/2 teaspoon salt
1 teaspoon pepper

To prepare the coleslaw, combine the cabbage, carrot, green pepper, celery and green onions in a large salad bowl and mix gently.

To prepare the dressing, combine the mayonnaise, sour cream, sugar, vinegar, mustard, paprika, salt and pepper in a small bowl and mix well. Add to the cabbage mixture and toss gently to coat evenly. Chill, covered, for 2 hours or longer.

Serves eight to ten

BLACK BEAN AND ROASTED RED PEPPER SALAD

6 (15-ounce) cans black beans
1 (12-ounce) jar roasted red peppers
1 cup rice vinegar
1/4 cup extra-virgin olive oil
2 tablespoons honey
1/2 teaspoon crushed hot chile flakes
1/2 cup minced fresh cilantro or parsley
1/4 cup chopped green onions
　　salt and pepper to taste
　　cilantro sprigs

Rinse and drain the beans well. Drain the roasted peppers and chop coarsely. Combine the beans and roasted peppers with the rice vinegar, olive oil, honey and chile flakes in a bowl and mix well. Chill, covered, until serving time or finish and serve immediately.

To finish, add the minced cilantro and green onions to the salad and toss to mix well. Season with salt and pepper and garnish with the cilantro sprigs.

Serves fifteen

HEARTS OF PALM SALAD

Spicy Onion Dressing

1/4	small onion, chopped
3	tablespoons cider vinegar
2	teaspoons spicy brown mustard
1/2	teaspoon sugar
1/2	teaspoon salt
1/4	teaspoon pepper
1	cup vegetable oil

Salad

13	ounces bacon
1	(7-ounce) can hearts of palm
1	(8-ounce) can artichoke hearts
2	bunches romaine lettuce, torn
1	cup (4 ounces) crumbled blue cheese

To prepare the dressing, combine the onion and vinegar in a blender and process until the onion is puréed. Add the mustard, sugar, salt and pepper and blend until smooth. Add the vegetable oil gradually, processing constantly at high speed until thickened.

To prepare the salad, fry the bacon in a skillet over medium heat until crisp. Drain, cool and crumble the bacon. Drain and chop the hearts of palm. Drain the artichoke hearts and cut into quarters. Combine the hearts of palm, artichoke hearts, romaine, blue cheese and bacon in a large bowl and toss to mix. Add the dressing at serving time and toss to coat evenly.
Serves six to eight

TO **MAKE CROUTONS,** *cut four 1/2-inch slices of French bread into cubes. Melt 1/4 cup butter in a skillet and remove from the heat. Stir in 1/8 teaspoon garlic powder and the bread cubes, coating well. Spread in a single layer on a baking sheet and bake at 300 degrees for 10 minutes. Stir and bake for 5 minutes longer or until dry and crisp. You may add herbs and Parmesan cheese for variety if desired.*

GREEK SALAD

Greek Dressing

1/2	cup olive oil
1/4	cup vinegar
1	large garlic clove, minced
2	tablespoons chopped fresh parsley
	pinch of dried oregano leaves
	salt and freshly ground pepper to taste

Salad

4	or 5 medium tomatoes, cut into wedges
1	medium cucumber, sliced diagonally
1	small green bell pepper, thinly sliced
5	green onions, sliced
5	radishes, sliced
15	marinated green or black Greek olives
1/2	cup (2 ounces) crumbled feta cheese
1/2	to 1 small head romaine, torn
2	tablespoons chopped fresh dill, or 2 teaspoons dillweed

To prepare the dressing, combine the olive oil, vinegar, garlic, parsley, oregano, salt and pepper in a sealable container and shake to mix well. Chill in the refrigerator for several days if possible to enhance the flavors.

To prepare the salad, combine the tomatoes, cucumber, green pepper, green onions, radishes, olives and feta cheese in a bowl and mix well. Add the romaine, dill and dressing and toss to coat well.

You may substitute other greens for the romaine in the salad or add the vegetables of your choice. You may add a pinch of sugar to the dressing if it is too tart for your taste.

Serves eight

MANDARIN ORANGE SALAD

Feta and Almond Topping

1/3	cup (1 1/3 ounces) crumbled feta cheese
1/2	cup sliced or slivered almonds
3	tablespoons sugar

Balsamic Dressing

1/4	cup olive oil
2	tablespoons balsamic vinegar
2	dashes Tabasco sauce
2	tablespoons sugar
1	tablespoon parsley flakes
1/2	tablespoon salt
1/2	tablespoon pepper

Salad

1/2	head green leaf lettuce, torn
1/2	head red leaf lettuce, torn
1	cup chopped celery (optional)
2	green onions, chopped
1	(11-ounce) can mandarin oranges, drained
1/2	cup dried cranberries

To prepare the topping, combine the feta cheese, almonds and sugar in a baking pan and mix well. Broil until the mixture has caramelized. Let stand until cool.

To prepare the dressing, combine the olive oil, balsamic vinegar and Tabasco sauce in a jar. Add the sugar, parsley flakes, salt and pepper and shake to dissolve the sugar and salt completely.

To prepare the salad, combine the green leaf lettuce, red leaf lettuce, celery and green onions in a salad bowl. Add the mandarin oranges and dried cranberries and mix gently. Add the dressing and toss to coat evenly. Spoon onto serving plates and sprinkle with the topping.
Serves four to six

SPINACH SALAD WITH
WARM BACON DRESSING

Salad

1	(9-ounce) package fresh baby spinach
1/2	cup sliced red onion
1/2	cup sweetened dried cranberries
1/2	cup walnuts, toasted

Bacon Dressing

6	slices bacon
1/2	cup cider vinegar
2	tablespoons olive oil
2	teaspoons Dijon mustard
1	tablespoon sugar
1/2	teaspoon pepper

To prepare the salad, combine the spinach with the onion, cranberries and walnuts in a serving bowl. Set aside.

To prepare the dressing, fry the bacon in a skillet over medium heat until crisp. Remove to paper towels and drain all but 1 tablespoon bacon drippings from the skillet. Crumble the bacon.

Add the vinegar, olive oil, Dijon mustard, sugar and pepper to the skillet and mix well. Cook over medium-low heat for 1 minute. Pour over the salad and toss to coat evenly. Top with the crumbled bacon. Serve immediately.

Serves six to eight

SPRING SALAD WITH
APPLE CIDER DRESSING

Apple Cider Dressing

1/3	cup apple cider vinegar
1	cup vegetable oil
2	tablespoons honey
3/4	cup sugar
1	tablespoon grated onion
1	teaspoon minced garlic
1	teaspoon dry mustard
1/2	teaspoon salt
	pepper to taste

Salad

4	cups spring greens
4	or 5 slices red onion, separated into rings
1	green apple, chopped
1/3	cup (1 1/3 ounces) crumbled blue cheese
1/3	cup dried cranberries or dried cherries
1/3	cup toasted walnuts or pecans

To prepare the dressing, combine the apple cider vinegar, vegetable oil and honey in a jar. Add the sugar, onion, garlic, dry mustard, salt and pepper and shake to mix well.

To prepare the salad, combine the greens with the onion, apple, blue cheese, cranberries and walnuts in a large bowl. Add 1 cup of the dressing and toss to coat evenly.

Store the remaining dressing in an airtight container in the refrigerator.

Serves six

PECAN CRUNCH *is a wonderful topping for any salad, or even served alone as a snack. Combine 2/3 cup chopped pecans, 2 tablespoons butter, 1 tablespoon sugar, 1/2 teaspoon salt, 1/4 teaspoon cayenne pepper, and freshly ground black pepper to taste in a saucepan. Cook until the mixture caramelizes. Transfer to a small paper bag to cool, shaking occasionally to break up. The mixture can be stored in an airtight container or frozen for up to one month. The recipe can be doubled or tripled.*

WINTER SALAD

Cherry Dressing

1 1/4   cups dried tart cherries
1/2   cup tawny port
5   ounces pancetta or bacon, chopped
2   shallots, minced
1   garlic clove, minced
1/3   cup olive oil
1/4   cup red wine vinegar
2   teaspoons sugar
        salt and pepper to taste

Salad

1   (5 1/2-inch) log soft fresh goat cheese
1   (5-ounce) package mixed salad greens
1/2   cup pine nuts, toasted

To prepare the dressing, combine the cherries and port in a small heavy saucepan and bring to a boil over medium heat. Remove from the heat and let stand for 15 minutes or until the cherries are plump.

Sauté the pancetta in a large heavy skillet over medium-low heat until crisp. Add the shallots and garlic and sauté for 2 minutes. Add the olive oil, vinegar and sugar and cook until the sugar dissolves completely, stirring constantly. Stir in the cherry mixture and season with salt and pepper.

To prepare the salad, cut the goat cheese into 1/2-inch slices and arrange in a baking pan. Bake at 350 degrees for 10 minutes. Combine the salad greens and pine nuts in a salad bowl. Pour the warm dressing over the salad and toss gently to coat well. Top with the warm goat cheese and serve immediately.

You may prepare the dressing in advance and hold at room temperature for up to 2 hours. Reheat to serve.

Serves four

CARIBBEAN WATERCRESS SALAD

Cilantro Dressing

1/2	cup extra-virgin olive oil
3	tablespoons fresh lime juice
	leaves of 1/2 bunch cilantro
1	garlic clove, minced
	salt and pepper to taste

Salad

2	bunches watercress
1	red grapefruit, peeled and sliced
1	orange, peeled and sliced
1	tomato, cut into quarters

To prepare the dressing, combine the olive oil, lime juice, cilantro, garlic, salt and pepper in a blender and process until smooth.

To prepare the salad, combine the watercress, grapefruit, orange and tomato in a salad bowl. Add 1/3 cup of the dressing and toss to coat well. Chill until serving time.

Store the unused portion of the salad dressing in the refrigerator for another use.

Serves four

HERBED POLENTA CROUTONS

5	cups chicken broth
1	teaspoon salt
12/3	cups uncooked polenta or stone-ground cornmeal
2	tablespoons butter
1/3	cup (11/3 ounces) grated Parmesan cheese
2	tablespoons minced fresh herbs
	butter or olive oil

Bring the chicken broth and salt to a boil in a saucepan. Whisk in the polenta gradually and return the mixture to a boil. Reduce the heat and simmer for 15 minutes, stirring constantly. Remove from the heat and stir in 2 tablespoons butter, Parmesan cheese and herbs. Pour into a buttered 9×13-inch dish and let stand until cool. Chill in the refrigerator for 8 hours or longer.

Dip the dish in hot water to loosen the polenta and invert onto a cutting board. Cut into stars or other shapes with a cutter. Add enough butter or olive oil to a skillet to coat the bottom and heat over medium–high heat. Add the polenta shapes and sauté for 2 minutes on each side or until heated through and light golden brown. Remove to paper towels to drain. Add to salads for a special presentation.

Serves six

The photograph for this recipe is on the cover.

FRUIT SALAD WITH
AMARETTO CREAM SAUCE

Amaretto Cream Sauce

1/2   cup heavy cream
2   egg yolks
1/4   cup sugar
1/2   cup Amaretto

Salad

1   cup raspberries
1   cup blueberries
1   cup strawberries, cut into halves
1/2   cup chopped orange sections
1/2   cup chopped grapefruit sections
1/2   cup chopped Granny Smith apples
1/2   cup green seedless grapes
1/2   cup chopped peaches
1/2   cup chopped apricots
   juice of 1/2 lemon
1/2   cup sugar
2   tablespoons chopped mint

To prepare the sauce, bring the cream to a boil in a saucepan. Whisk the egg yolks with the sugar in a small bowl. Whisk a small amount of the hot cream into the egg yolk mixture; then whisk the egg yolk mixture into the hot cream. Cook for 2 minutes, stirring constantly. Strain into a small pitcher and stir in the liqueur. Cool to room temperature or chill until serving time.

To prepare the salad, combine the raspberries, blueberries, strawberries, oranges, grapefruit, apples, grapes, peaches, apricots, lemon juice, sugar and mint in a large bowl and mix gently. Chill, covered, in the refrigerator for 8 hours or longer. Serve with the cream sauce.
Serves eight

ORANGE SOUFFLÉ

3	tablespoons unflavored gelatin
2	cups sugar
	pinch of salt
4	egg yolks
2 1/2	cups orange juice
3	tablespoons lemon juice
2	cups whipped cream
1	cup mandarin oranges

Mix the gelatin with the sugar and salt in a saucepan. Beat the egg yolks with 1 cup of the orange juice in a bowl. Add to the gelatin mixture and mix well. Let stand for 5 minutes to soften the gelatin. Bring to a boil over medium heat, stirring until the gelatin and sugar dissolve completely.

Remove from the heat and add the remaining 1 1/2 cups orange juice and lemon juice. Pour into a bowl placed in a larger bowl filled with water and ice cubes. Let stand until syrupy, stirring frequently. Remove from the ice water bath and fold in the whipped cream.

Arrange the oranges in a decorative mold, individual molds or a soufflé dish. Spoon in the gelatin mixture. Chill until very firm. Dip the mold briefly into hot water to loosen the gelatin and invert onto a serving plate.

Serves ten to twelve

GRAPEFRUIT AND AVOCADO SALAD

2	large Texas ruby red grapefruit
3	avocados
	lettuce leaves
	poppy seed dressing

Peel the grapefruit, removing all the white pith. Hold the grapefruit over a bowl and slice along the edge of a section down to the center of the fruit. Turn the knife to slide the section out of the membrane whole. Repeat until all the sections are removed.

Cut each avocado into halves, discarding the seeds. Cut each half into halves and cut each into 2 or 3 slices, cutting to but not through the skin. Scoop the slices gently from the skin with a spoon. Combine with the grapefruit sections in the bowl, tossing gently to coat well with the grapefruit juice to keep the avocados from turning brown. Spoon the mixture onto serving plates lined with lettuce leaves and drizzle with poppy seed dressing.

Serves four

PEAR AND RED POTATO SALAD

Curried Chutney Dressing

1/4	cup rice vinegar
1	teaspoon sugar
1	teaspoon Dijon mustard
1	teaspoon curry powder
	salt and freshly ground pepper to taste
1/2	cup fruity olive oil
3	green onions with tops, sliced diagonally
1/4	cup chutney

Salad

1	cup rock salt
2	pounds small red potatoes
3	pears, peeled and cut into quarters
1	head butter lettuce
1/4	cup chopped pistachios

To prepare the dressing, combine the vinegar, sugar, Dijon mustard, curry powder, salt and pepper in a small jar. Shake to mix well. Add the olive oil and shake to blend. Add the green onions and chutney and shake again.

To prepare the salad, spread the rock salt in a large baking pan and arrange the potatoes in the salt. Roast at 375 degrees for 15 to 20 minutes or until the potatoes are tender. Remove the potatoes from the salt bed and cool.

Slice the potatoes and combine with the pears in a large bowl. Add the dressing and toss gently. Spoon into a shallow salad bowl lined with the lettuce leaves and sprinkle with the pistachios.

Serves eight

RUBY RED GRAPEFRUIT *from Texas has earned a reputation as the world's most delicious grapefruit. This red-fleshed grapefruit will attain the perfect sweetness when allowed to ripen on the tree. When selecting a grapefruit, look for one that seems heavy for its size. The skin should be smooth and blemish free, although a few surface scratches or slight greening of the skin will not affect the quality of the fruit.*

ROASTED POTATO SALAD

4   cups quartered small red potatoes with skins
2   hard-cooked eggs, chopped
1   cup mayonnaise
4   slices bacon, crisp-fried and crumbled
1/4 cup sliced green onions
1/4 teaspoon salt
1/4 teaspoon pepper

Spread the potatoes in a single layer on a large baking sheet sprayed with nonstick cooking spray. Roast at 425 degrees for 30 to 35 minutes or until tender, stirring halfway through the baking time.

Combine the eggs, mayonnaise, bacon, green onions, salt and pepper in a large bowl. Add the potatoes and toss lightly to coat well. Serve warm.

You may also allow the potatoes to cool before mixing with the salad ingredients and chill the salad before serving.

Serves six

CORN BREAD SALAD

Lime Dressing

3   tablespoons olive oil
1   tablespoon white vinegar
6   tablespoons fresh lime juice

Salad

3   cups prepared, dried and coarsely crumbled corn bread
1/2 red bell pepper, chopped
1/2 green bell pepper, chopped
1/2 red onion, chopped
4   green onions, chopped
1   (4-ounce) can chopped green chiles, drained
4   garlic cloves, minced
1/4 cup chopped fresh cilantro
1   tablespoon cumin seeds
     salt and cracked pepper to taste

To prepare the dressing, combine the olive oil, vinegar and lime juice in a small bowl and whisk to blend well.

To prepare the salad, combine the corn bread, red bell pepper, green bell pepper, red onion, green onions, green chiles, garlic and cilantro in a large bowl and mix lightly. Add the cumin seeds, salt and pepper and toss. Add the dressing and toss to coat evenly. Serve immediately.

Serves six to eight

MEDITERRANEAN COUSCOUS SALAD

Lemon Oregano Vinaigrette

3   tablespoons lemon juice
2   tablespoons olive oil
1   tablespoon chopped fresh mint, or 1/4 teaspoon crushed dried mint
1   tablespoon chopped fresh oregano, or 3/4 teaspoon crushed dried oregano

Salad

1 3/4   cups water
1   cup quick-cooking couscous
1   medium red bell pepper, chopped
1/2   cup seeded and chopped cucumber
1/4   cup sliced or chopped black Greek olives
1/4   cup (1 ounce) crumbled feta cheese
      Pita Chips (page 65) or crisp crackers

   To prepare the vinaigrette, combine the lemon juice, olive oil, mint and oregano in a jar and shake to mix well.

   To prepare the salad, bring the water to a boil in a saucepan and remove from the heat. Stir in the couscous and cover. Let stand for 5 minutes; fluff with a fork.

   Remove to a bowl and drizzle with the vinaigrette. Cool for 10 minutes. Add the bell pepper, cucumber and olives and toss gently to mix well. Sprinkle with the feta cheese. Serve with Pita Chips or crisp crackers.

Serves four

CHA-CHA CHICKEN SALAD

4   chicken breasts, grilled and chopped
      salt and pepper to taste
1   (16-ounce) package coleslaw with red cabbage and carrots
1 1/2   cups red grape halves
1   cup sliced strawberries
1   cup blueberries
1   cup walnuts, broken
1   cup poppy seed dressing
      lettuce

   Sprinkle the chicken with salt and pepper in a bowl. Add the coleslaw, grapes, strawberries, blueberries and walnuts. Add the poppy seed dressing and toss to coat well. Serve on a bed of lettuce.

Serves six

CURRIED CHICKEN SALAD

Curry Dijon Dressing

2	tablespoons pineapple juice drained from the sliced pineapple in the salad
2/3	cup mayonnaise
1	tablespoon Dijon mustard
3/4	teaspoon curry powder
	salt to taste

Salad

4	large chicken breasts, cooked and slivered
1/4	cup thinly sliced celery
2	tablespoons thinly sliced green onions
1/3	cup slivered almonds, toasted
1/3	cup raisins
	lettuce leaves
4	to 6 pineapple slices
	seedless green or red grape halves

To prepare the dressing, combine the pineapple juice, mayonnaise, Dijon mustard, curry powder and salt in a bowl and mix until smooth.

To prepare the salad, combine the chicken, celery, green onions, almonds and raisins in a bowl and mix well. Add the dressing and toss to coat well. Chill, covered, for 1 hour or longer.

Arrange the lettuce leaves on serving plates and top with the pineapple slices. Spoon the chicken mixture onto the prepared plates and top with grapes.

Serves four to six

CREAM PUFFS *provide a great way to serve chicken salad. Combine 1 cup water with 1/2 cup butter and 1/8 teaspoon salt in a saucepan and bring to a boil. Add 1 cup flour and stir to mix well. Remove from the heat and cool for 10 minutes. Add 4 eggs 1 at a time, mixing until smooth after each addition. Drop by tablespoonfuls onto a greased baking sheet and bake at 400 degrees for 30 to 35 minutes or until golden brown. Cool, cut off the tops, and remove any inner filaments before filling with the salad.*

CHICKEN SALAD NIÇOISE

Salad

8	to 10 small red potatoes
1	tablespoon olive oil
4	large boneless skinless chicken breasts
	salt and pepper to taste
1	tablespoon olive oil
6	ounces penne or corkscrew pasta, cooked
3	medium plum tomatoes, chopped
1	bunch arugula or spinach
1/2	cup kalamata olives (optional)
1/2	cup (2 ounces) crumbled feta cheese or grated Parmesan cheese

Niçoise Dressing

	grated zest and juice of 1 medium lemon
1/2	teaspoon sugar
2	tablespoons olive oil
1	teaspoon salt
1/4	teaspoon pepper

To prepare the salad, cut the potatoes into 1-inch pieces and toss with 1 tablespoon olive oil in a bowl. Spread in a single layer in a baking pan and roast at 450 degrees for 25 minutes.

Sprinkle the chicken with the salt and pepper and sauté in 1 tablespoon olive oil in a skillet until cooked through. Drain and chop the chicken. Combine the chicken with the potatoes, pasta, tomatoes, arugula, olives and feta cheese in a bowl and mix gently.

To prepare the dressing, combine the lemon zest, lemon juice, sugar, olive oil, salt and pepper in a bowl and mix well. Add to the salad and toss to coat well. Chill in the refrigerator for 2 hours or longer. Serve with warm French bread.
Serves six

CHINESE CHICKEN SALAD

Sweet-and-Sour Vinaigrette

2	tablespoons vinegar
2	tablespoons sugar
1	teaspoon salt
1	teaspoon pepper
1/4	cup vegetable oil

Salad

2	chicken breasts
1/2	cup almonds
1/4	cup sesame seeds
1	tablespoon vegetable oil
1/4	(14-ounce) package rice sticks
2	green onions, chopped
1	head iceberg lettuce, torn

To prepare the vinaigrette, combine the vinegar, sugar, salt and pepper in a saucepan and mix well. Heat until the sugar dissolves completely, stirring constantly. Remove from the heat and cool. Add the vegetable oil; mix well.

To prepare the salad, cook the chicken in water in a saucepan until tender; drain. Cool and shred the chicken, discarding the skin and bones.

Toast the almonds and sesame seeds in the vegetable oil in a skillet until light brown, stirring constantly. Combine with the chicken, rice sticks, green onions and lettuce in a bowl. Add the vinaigrette and toss gently to coat evenly.

Serves ten to twelve

SHRIMP PASTA SALAD

Seasoned Dressing

1	cup mayonnaise
1	tablespoon white wine
1/2	teaspoon sugar
1/2	teaspoon onion powder
1/2	teaspoon garlic powder
1/2	teaspoon Italian seasoning
1/2	teaspoon basil
1/2	teaspoon nutmeg
1/2	teaspoon salt

Salad

8	ounces small shrimp, cooked
4	cups cooked bow tie or other small pasta
1	red bell pepper, chopped
1	cup chopped celery
1	bunch green onions, chopped

To prepare the dressing, combine the mayonnaise and wine in a bowl. Add the sugar, onion powder, garlic powder, Italian seasoning, basil, nutmeg and salt and whisk until smooth.

To prepare the salad, combine the shrimp, pasta, bell pepper, celery and green onions in a salad bowl. Add the dressing and toss to coat evenly. Chill, covered, for 1 hour or longer. Serve chilled.

Serves five

KEEP GREENS FRESH *with these simple steps. Soak the greens in cold water for a few minutes to perk them up and to rinse off the leaves. Drain well, preferably with a salad spinner. To maintain their crispness, spread the greens on paper towels and roll loosely before placing them in a sealable plastic bag. The paper towels will keep the water off the greens while keeping them moist.*

SHELLFISH-STUFFED AVOCADO SALAD

8	ounces lobster tail meat
8	ounces crawfish tails
8	ounces bay scallops
8	ounces gulf shrimp
1/2	cup chopped celery
1/2	cup chopped red bell pepper
1/4	cup chopped chives
1/2	bunch cilantro, chopped
5	fresh basil leaves, chopped
1	tablespoon chopped garlic
1/2	cup (2 ounces) crumbled feta cheese
	salt and pepper to taste
	spring mix greens
4	avocados, cut into halves
	crumbled feta cheese
16	tomatoes, cut into quarters
16	lemons, cut into quarters
	Greek vinaigrette

Steam or boil the lobster meat, crawfish tails, scallops and shrimp until cooked through. Drain and chill the shellfish.

Combine the celery, bell pepper, chives, cilantro, basil, garlic, 1/2 cup feta cheese, salt and pepper in a bowl and mix well. Add the shellfish and mix gently. Chill for 1 hour.

Arrange the spring mix greens on the serving plates and top each with an avocado half. Spoon the shellfish mixture into the avocados and sprinkle with additional feta cheese. Arrange the tomato wedges and lemon wedges around the avocados. Drizzle with Greek vinaigrette.

Serves eight

ASIAN GINGER DRESSING

1/2   cup pineapple juice
2   tablespoons cider vinegar
1   tablespoon soy sauce
1/2   teaspoon sesame oil
1   tablespoon sugar
1   teaspoon grated gingerroot

Combine the pineapple juice, cider vinegar, soy sauce and sesame oil in a jar. Add the sugar and gingerroot and shake to mix well and dissolve the sugar. Store in the refrigerator or serve immediately over green salads, chicken salad or pasta salad.
Serves four

HONEY DRESSING

2/3   cup sugar
1   teaspoon dry mustard
1   teaspoon celery salt
1/4   teaspoon salt
1/3   cup honey
1   tablespoon lemon juice
5   teaspoons vinegar
1   cup vegetable oil

Mix the sugar, dry mustard, celery salt and salt in a bowl. Add the honey, lemon juice and vinegar and mix well. Add the vegetable oil gradually, beating well until smooth.
Serves eight

POPPY SEED DRESSING

1/4   cup apple cider vinegar
1/4   teaspoon Worcestershire sauce
1/2   cup canola oil
1/2   cup sugar
1/4   teaspoon paprika
1 1/2 teaspoons finely chopped green onions
1   tablespoon poppy seeds

Combine the vinegar, Worcestershire sauce and canola oil in a jar. Add the sugar, paprika, green onions and poppy seeds and shake until the sugar dissolves.
Serves four to six

PERFECT VINAIGRETTE

1   medium shallot, finely chopped
2   tablespoons balsamic vinegar
1/2   teaspoon sea salt
1/3   to 1/2 cup extra-virgin olive oil

Combine the shallot with the balsamic vinegar and sea salt in a bowl and mix well. Let stand for 30 minutes. Whisk in the olive oil just before serving.
Serves four

CUCUMBER CHILL

4 1/2	medium cucumbers, peeled, seeded and chopped
1	large onion, chopped
1/4	cup (1/2 stick) margarine
1/4	cup flour
5	cups canned chicken broth
2	bay leaves
1/2	cup (4 ounces) sour cream
1/2	teaspoon Tabasco sauce
1/2	teaspoon dillweed
1	teaspoon salt
1	cup half-and-half
2	tablespoons lemon juice

Sauté the cucumbers and onion in the margarine in a saucepan until tender. Reduce the heat and stir in the flour gradually. Remove from the heat and cool for 1 minute. Stir in the chicken broth and bay leaves. Bring to a boil, stirring constantly. Reduce the heat and simmer for 30 minutes.

Pour the mixture into a blender and process until smooth. Combine with the sour cream, Tabasco sauce, dillweed and salt in a bowl and mix well. Cool to room temperature and chill in the refrigerator. Stir in the half-and-half and lemon juice and discard the bay leaves. Chill until serving time.

Serves six to eight

STRAWBERRY SOUP

2	cups strawberries
1	cup (8 ounces) strawberry yogurt
1/2	cup white wine

Combine the strawberries and yogurt in a blender or food processor and process until puréed. Add the wine and blend until smooth. Remove to a bowl and chill, covered, for 3 hours. Serve chilled.

Serves six

The photograph for this recipe is on page 13.

ROASTED CORN SOUP WITH CHIPOTLES

1	whole garlic head, roasted (see below)
1 1/2	cups fresh corn kernels, or 1 (10-ounce) package frozen corn, thawed
1	yellow onion, finely chopped
	vegetable oil
2	cups milk
1/4	teaspoon ground coriander
1/4	teaspoon ground cumin
1	teaspoon salt
1/4	teaspoon cayenne pepper
2	cups heavy cream
2	tablespoons puréed canned chipotle peppers in adobo sauce
	chopped scallions

Press the cloves from the head of garlic and chop or crush. Spread the corn on a baking sheet. Broil just until evenly browned, shaking the baking sheet frequently.

Sauté the onion and garlic in a small amount of heated vegetable oil in a heavy stockpot until the onion is translucent. Add the corn, milk, coriander, cumin, salt and cayenne pepper and mix well. Bring to a boil and reduce the heat. Stir in the cream and simmer for 15 minutes.

Remove the corn and onion from the soup to a blender or food processor with a slotted spoon. Add a small amount of the liquid from the soup and process until smooth. Return the purée to the soup. Add the chipotle peppers to the soup and simmer for 10 minutes longer. Ladle into serving bowls and garnish with scallions.

You may substitute dried chipotle peppers for the canned ones if preferred. Soak the dried peppers in hot water for 15 minutes, discard the seeds and stems and purée in a food processor.

Serves four

TO ROAST GARLIC, *remove some of the papery husk from the head of garlic, reserving the cloves intact. Slice off the top 1/4 inch from the head and rub the entire head with olive oil. Wrap in foil and roast at 350 degrees for 45 minutes. Cool before pressing out the individual cloves.*

CREAM OF JALAPEÑO SOUP

8	ounces fresh jalapeño peppers
1	cup milk
1/4	cup (1/2 stick) butter
1/2	small onion, finely chopped
3	garlic cloves, finely chopped
1/4	cup flour
3	cups hot chicken broth
2	tablespoons fresh lime juice
1	cup chopped cilantro
1 1/2	cups hot milk
	ground cumin to taste
	salt and pepper to taste
3/4	cup hot heavy cream
	chopped cilantro
	crisp-fried tortilla strips

Seed, devein and chop the jalapeño peppers wearing tight latex gloves. Soak the peppers in 1 cup milk in a bowl for 30 minutes.

Melt the butter in a heavy 5-quart saucepan. Drain the peppers and add to the saucepan with the onion and garlic. Sauté until the onion is tender-crisp but not brown. Add the flour and cook for 3 to 4 minutes or until bubbly, stirring constantly. Whisk in the hot broth and cook until thickened, whisking constantly. Whisk in the lime juice and 1 cup cilantro.

Process the soup in batches in a blender until smooth. Combine the purée batches in the saucepan and add 1 1/2 cups hot milk, or enough to make of the desired consistency. Heat just to the simmering point. Season with cumin, salt and pepper. Add the cream just before serving.

Ladle into soup bowls and garnish with additional chopped cilantro and crisp tortilla strips.
Serves four

The photograph for this recipe is on page 83.

FRENCH ONION SOUP

4	medium onions, thinly sliced
1/4	cup (1/2 stick) butter
4	cups beef broth
1/4	cup Cognac
2	tablespoons molasses
1	teaspoon Worcestershire sauce
3/4	teaspoon salt
	toasted bread slices
	shredded or sliced mozzarella cheese

Sauté the onions in the butter in a heavy saucepan until translucent. Add the beef broth, Cognac, molasses, Worcestershire sauce and salt and mix well. Bring to a boil and reduce the heat. Simmer for 2 to 3 hours or until of the desired consistency. Ladle into soup bowls and top each with a slice of toasted bread. Sprinkle the bread with the shredded cheese.

You may also ladle the soup into ovenproof bowls, top with the toast and sliced cheese and broil until the cheese is golden brown and bubbly.
Serves four to six

BAKED POTATO SOUP

6   green onions, chopped
4   pounds baking potatoes, baked
6   ounces bacon
3   cups finely chopped yellow onions
1 1/2   cups finely chopped celery
2   cups finely chopped carrots
2   teaspoons finely chopped garlic
2   teaspoons seasoned salt
2   teaspoons white pepper
2   teaspoons cracked black pepper
4   cups heavy cream
3   to 4 cups chicken stock
2   tablespoons butter
2   tablespoons flour
2   cups (8 ounces) shredded Cheddar cheese

Reserve 2 tablespoons of the green onions for garnish. Peel the baked potatoes and cut into 1/2-inch pieces. Cut the bacon into 1/4-inch strips.

Heat an 8- to 10-inch saucepan over high heat for 2 to 3 minutes. Add the bacon and cook until the drippings are rendered and the bacon is light brown, stirring frequently. Reserve 2 tablespoons of the bacon for garnish.

Reduce the heat to medium-high and add the chopped onions, remaining green onions, celery, carrots, garlic, seasoned salt, white pepper and cracked pepper to the drippings in the saucepan. Sauté until the vegetables are light brown. Add the potatoes and sauté for 5 minutes longer or until the vegetable mixture appears dry, stirring gently. Add the heavy cream and 3 cups of the chicken stock and bring to a simmer.

Heat a 6- to 10-inch sauté pan over medium-low heat. Add the butter and heat until the butter melts. Stir in the flour and cook for 2 to 3 minutes or until bubbly and golden brown, stirring occasionally. Add to the soup and cook for 2 to 3 minutes or until well mixed, stirring gently to avoid breaking up the potatoes.

Reduce the heat and simmer for 15 minutes, stirring occasionally and adding the remaining 1 cup chicken stock if necessary for the desired consistency. Stir in 1 cup of the Cheddar cheese. Ladle into heated soup bowls and top the servings with the remaining 1 cup cheese and the reserved green onions and bacon.
Serves eight

BAKED SQUASH BISQUE

2	acorn squash
4	teaspoons butter
1	cup minced onion
1/4	cup minced carrot
3	tablespoons butter
4	cups chicken broth
2	medium potatoes, peeled and chopped
1/2	teaspoon salt
1/2	teaspoon pepper
1/2	cup milk
1/2	cup heavy cream
1/4	teaspoon cayenne pepper

Cut the squash into halves lengthwise and scoop out the seeds. Place cut side up on a baking sheet and place 1 teaspoon butter in the cavity of each half. Bake at 350 degrees for 2 hours or until fork-tender. Cool to room temperature and scoop the pulp into a bowl, discarding the shells.

Sauté the onion and carrot in 3 tablespoons butter in a heavy saucepan until the onion is translucent. Add the chicken broth, potatoes, salt and pepper and cook until the potatoes are tender.

Combine the squash pulp with the chicken broth mixture in a food processor and process at low speed until smooth. Add the milk and cream and process until well mixed. Return to the saucepan and cook until heated through. Ladle into soup bowls and sprinkle with the cayenne pepper.

Serves eight

BARLEY AND VEGETABLE SOUP WITH HAM

10	cups chicken broth
1	cup uncooked pearl barley
1/4	cup (1/2 stick) unsalted butter
1	large yellow onion, chopped
1	medium rib celery, thinly sliced
2	medium carrots, peeled and thinly sliced
5	ounces baked or boiled ham, chopped
1	bay leaf
1/2	cup half-and-half
1/2	cup (2 ounces) grated Parmigiano-Reggiano cheese
	salt and freshly ground pepper to taste

Bring the chicken broth to a boil in a large saucepan over medium-high heat. Add the barley and reduce the heat to medium-low. Cook, covered, for 1 hour or until the barley is tender.

Melt the butter in a large skillet over medium heat. Add the onion, celery, carrots, ham and bay leaf and sauté for 10 minutes or until the onion begins to brown. Add the mixture to the barley, scraping the skillet with a rubber spatula to deglaze. Simmer, covered, over medium heat for 20 minutes or until the vegetables are tender.

Add the half-and-half and cheese and cook until the cheese melts, stirring to mix well. Season to taste and discard the bay leaf before serving.

Serves six

A WARM BREAD BOWL *full of hot soup will warm up someone's heart.*

Cut off the top of a round loaf of sourdough bread and hollow it out, taking care not to pierce the shell. Brush the inside with olive oil and toast at 350 degrees for 10 minutes or until crusty. Ladle in the hot soup and serve immediately.

CHILI BLANCO

2	cups dried Great Northern beans
3	whole skinless chicken breasts
3¹/2	cups water
2	tablespoons olive oil
2	cups finely chopped onions
4	garlic cloves, minced
6	Anaheim peppers, roasted, peeled, seeded and chopped, or 2 (4-ounce) cans chopped green chiles
1	jalapeño pepper, seeded and chopped
2	(10-ounce) cans diced tomatoes with green chiles
2	teaspoons ground cumin
1	tablespoon minced fresh oregano, or 1 teaspoon dried oregano
¹/4	teaspoon cayenne pepper
3	cups chicken stock
	salt to taste
2	cups (8 ounces) shredded Monterey Jack cheese
	chopped tomatoes, chopped green onions, chopped cilantro, shredded Monterey Jack cheese and/or chopped jalapeño peppers

Combine the beans with enough water to cover in a large saucepan and soak for 1 hour. Combine the chicken with 3¹/2 cups water in a large covered saucepan. Bring to a low simmer and cook for 30 minutes or until the chicken is cooked through. Remove the chicken, reserving the broth, and cool the chicken. Shred into bite-size pieces, discarding the bones.

Drain the beans and set aside. Heat the olive oil in the saucepan over medium heat. Add the onions and sauté for 10 minutes or until translucent. Add the garlic, Anaheim peppers, 1 jalapeño pepper, tomatoes with green chiles, cumin, oregano and cayenne pepper and cook for several minutes.

Add the beans, reserved chicken broth and chicken stock and bring to a boil. Reduce the heat and simmer, covered, for 2 hours or until the beans are tender, stirring occasionally. Season with salt to taste.

Stir in the chicken and 2 cups Monterey Jack cheese before serving and cook until the cheese melts and the soup is heated through. Ladle into serving bowls and garnish with chopped tomatoes, green onions, cilantro and additional cheese and jalapeño peppers.

You may substitute 4 cans Great Northern beans for the dried beans and reduce the cooking time accordingly if preferred.

Serves six

TEXAS CHILI

5   pounds lean beef, coarsely ground for chili
2   white onions, finely chopped
3   tablespoons minced garlic
8   or 9 ounces green chiles, chopped
1/2 cup regular chili powder
1   tablespoon Mexican hot chili powder
1   tablespoon Texas-style chili powder
2   or 3 drops of Tabasco sauce
2   tablespoons ground cumin
2   teaspoons salt
1/2 tablespoon ground red pepper
2   teaspoons black pepper
3   (15-ounce) cans tomato sauce
     shredded cheese and chopped onion

Brown the ground beef in a large saucepan over medium heat, stirring until crumbly; drain the excess drippings. Add 2 onions and the garlic and sauté just until the onions are translucent.

Add the green chiles, regular chili powder, Mexican hot chili powder, Texas-style chili powder, Tabasco sauce, cumin, salt, red pepper and black pepper and mix well. Simmer over medium heat for 30 to 45 minutes to blend the flavors, stirring to prevent sticking; do not boil.

Stir in the tomato sauce and reduce the heat. Cook, covered, for 2 to 3 hours or until of the desired consistency. Ladle into serving bowls and top with cheese and additional onion.

Remember that Texas chili is never made with beans.

Serves ten

ITALIAN SAUSAGE SOUP

1¹/₂ pounds ground sweet or spicy Italian sausage
1 cup chopped onion
2 garlic cloves, chopped
5 cups beef broth
1 cup red wine
1¹/₂ cups water
2 (16-ounce) cans stewed tomatoes
1 (8-ounce) can tomato sauce
1 cup sliced carrots
¹/₂ teaspoon basil
¹/₂ teaspoon oregano
1¹/₂ cups sliced zucchini
1 cup chopped green bell pepper
3 tablespoons chopped parsley
12 ounces uncooked cheese tortellini

Sauté the Italian sausage, onion and garlic in a large saucepan, stirring until the sausage is brown and crumbly; drain. Add the beef broth, red wine, water, tomatoes, tomato sauce, carrots, basil and oregano. Bring to a boil and reduce the heat. Simmer for 1¹/₄ hours.

Add the zucchini, green pepper, parsley and tortellini. Simmer for 45 minutes longer. Ladle into soup bowls and serve with a salad and garlic bread.

Serves six to eight

NACHOS *do not have to be reserved for Mexican meals; Italian Nachos are just as tasty. To prepare, just split 6 to 8 pita bread rounds and cut each layer into 4 wedges. Spread margarine or butter on the inner sides and sprinkle with dried basil leaves and grated Parmesan cheese. Arrange on a baking sheet and toast at 375 degrees for 4 to 8 minutes or until light brown.*

BLACK BEAN AND CHICKEN SOUP

1 1/2   pounds boneless skinless chicken breasts
3   tablespoons olive oil
1/2   cup chopped onion
2   garlic cloves, minced
1   teaspoon ground cumin
1/2   teaspoon chili powder
1/2   teaspoon salt
1/8   teaspoon ground red pepper
4   cups chicken broth
3   (15-ounce) cans whole kernel corn
3   (15-ounce) cans black beans, drained
1   (15-ounce) can Mexican stewed tomatoes
1   cup Mexican-style tomatoes with green chiles
1   bunch cilantro, chopped
        thinly sliced Monterey Pepper Jack cheese

Slice or chop the chicken into bite-size pieces. Heat the olive oil in a large saucepan and add the chicken, onion, garlic, cumin, chili powder, salt and red pepper. Sauté until the chicken is cooked through.

Stir in the chicken broth, undrained corn, black beans, stewed tomatoes and tomatoes with green chiles. Bring to a boil and reduce the heat. Simmer for 15 minutes.

Ladle the soup into soup bowls and sprinkle the servings with cilantro. Top with the Monterey Pepper Jack cheese.

Serves twelve to fourteen

FIESTA CHICKEN SOUP

1	medium onion, chopped
2	or 3 garlic cloves, crushed
1	tablespoon vegetable oil
3	cups chopped cooked chicken
1	(15-ounce) can stewed tomatoes
6	cups chicken broth
1	(10-ounce) can tomato soup
2	teaspoons Worcestershire sauce
	Tabasco sauce to taste
	pinch of sugar
1	teaspoon ground cumin
1	teaspoon chili powder
1	teaspoon salt
1/2	teaspoon pepper
3	avocados, chopped
	corn tortilla chips
	shredded Cheddar cheese
	lime juice to taste

Sauté the onion and garlic in the vegetable oil in a large saucepan. Add the chicken, tomatoes, chicken broth, tomato soup, Worcestershire sauce, Tabasco sauce, sugar, cumin, chili powder, salt and pepper and mix well. Simmer, uncovered, over low heat for 1 to 1 1/2 hours or until of the desired consistency.

Ladle into soup bowls and top with the avocados, tortilla chips and Cheddar cheese. You may also add lime juice to taste.

You may prepare this soup in a slow cooker if preferred. Simmer on Low for 4 hours or longer.

Serves six to eight

SHRIMP BISQUE

1	cup dry white wine or chicken broth
2	tablespoons cocktail sauce
1	(8-ounce) bottle of clam juice
1	teaspoon lemon juice
1	teaspoon Worcestershire sauce
1	teaspoon butter or margarine
1	teaspoon celery seeds
1	teaspoon paprika
1	teaspoon salt
1	teaspoon white pepper
1	pound uncooked medium shrimp, peeled and deveined
3	cups half-and-half
1/2	cup sherry

Combine the white wine, cocktail sauce, clam juice, lemon juice, Worcestershire sauce, butter, celery seeds, paprika, salt and white pepper in a heavy 4-quart saucepan. Bring to a boil and stir in the shrimp. Reduce the heat and simmer, uncovered, for 2 to 3 minutes or until the shrimp are cooked through.

Add the half-and-half gradually and cook just until heated through, stirring constantly; do not boil. Stir in the sherry just before serving.

Thaw frozen shrimp before adding to the bisque.

Serves four

SHRIMP GAZPACHO

1   (14-ounce) can diced tomatoes, drained
1   (29-ounce) can tomato sauce
1³/₄ cups water
2   tablespoons olive oil
1   tablespoon white or cider vinegar
3   tablespoons Worcestershire sauce
      juice of ¹/₂ lime
²/₃   cucumber, peeled and chopped
²/₃   green bell pepper, chopped
1   to 1¹/₂ serrano peppers with seeds, minced
2   ribs celery, chopped
2   or 3 cloves garlic, minced
1   medium onion, chopped
¹/₄   to ¹/₂ cup minced cilantro
¹/₂   tablespoon coarsely ground pepper
1¹/₂ pounds small to medium shrimp, cooked, peeled and deveined
2   or 3 avocados, sliced

Combine the tomatoes, tomato sauce, water, olive oil, vinegar, Worcestershire sauce and lime juice in a large bowl and mix well. Add the cucumber, green pepper, serrano peppers, celery, garlic, onion, cilantro and pepper and mix gently. Chill, covered, in the refrigerator for 12 to 24 hours.

Place the shrimp and avocados in the serving bowls and ladle the gazpacho into the bowls. Serve with breadsticks or crunchy garlic Parmesan bread.

Serves six

STAR ATTRACTIONS

WILD MUSHROOM AND
GOAT CHEESE QUESADILLAS

The H-E-B Grocery Corporation was looking for a grand idea that would redefine the idea of the traditional supermarket and change the way people shop for groceries. That idea came to life in 1994, when Central Market opened in Austin. Today, Central Market, a destination fresh market, is THE place for people who are passionate about food. The interior was designed to involve the customer in a serpentine-flow, full-view, European-style market experience. Here, one discovers the energy, color, and aroma of coffees, hot baked breads, vegetables, fruits, and herbs—some locally grown and others from as far away as Tanzania. There are now seven Central Market locations, including three in the Dallas Metroplex.

8	ounces mixed shiitake, crimini and oyster mushrooms, sliced
1/4	cup julienned red bell pepper
1/4	cup julienned green bell pepper
2	tablespoons olive oil
1	teaspoon chopped garlic
2	tablespoons sliced green onions
13/4	cups (7 ounces) crumbled goat cheese
8	Central Market Southwestern flour tortillas
	Central Market Mango Salsa
	guacamole

Sauté the mushrooms, red bell pepper and green bell pepper in the olive oil in a skillet for 4 to 5 minutes or until the bell peppers are tender. Add the garlic and green onions and sauté for 2 minutes longer. Remove from the heat and stir in the goat cheese.

Spread 3 heaping tablespoons of the mushroom mixture over 4 tortillas and top with the remaining tortillas. Grill on both sides on a flat griddle or in a large skillet until golden brown. Cut each quesadilla into 6 wedges. Serve with Central Market Mango Salsa and guacamole. *Serves six*

Central Market
SM
H·E·B

SINGAPORE STREET NOODLES

PF Chang's China Bistro features foods from the five culinary regions of China. Although its menu offers all the traditional Chinese favorites, lettuce wraps have become wildly popular and virtually synonymous with PF Chang's.

Singapore Sauce

2	tablespoons light vinegar
1/4	cup Madras curry powder
	pinch of turmeric (optional)
1/4	cup lite Kikkoman soy sauce
1	cup vegetarian oyster sauce
1/4	cup srircha chili sauce
1/4	cup ketchup

Noodles

2	gallons water
1	(1-pound) package rice stick noodles
1/4	cup canola oil
8	ounces medium shrimp, peeled
8	ounces boneless skinless chicken, julienned
1	tablespoon chopped garlic
1	cup julienned cabbage
1/2	cup julienned carrot
2	medium tomatoes, coarsely chopped
1	cup Singapore Sauce
	green portions of 1 bunch scallions, cut into 2-inch lengths
1/4	bunch cilantro, coarsely chopped
1	teaspoon sesame oil
1/3	cup fried chopped shallots (optional)
1	lime, cut into quarters

To prepare the sauce, combine the vinegar with the curry powder and turmeric in a bowl and mix to dissolve the spices. Add the soy sauce, oyster sauce, chili sauce and ketchup and mix well. Remove 1 cup of the sauce for the noodle recipe and reserve the remaining sauce for another use.

To prepare the noodles, bring the water to a rolling boil in a saucepan and stir in the rice stick noodles. Cook for 2 minutes or just until softened. Drain in a colander and rinse under rapidly running hot water for 1 minute; drain again. Toss with 2 tablespoons of the canola oil.

Heat the remaining 2 tablespoons canola oil in a wok and add the shrimp and chicken. Stir-fry for 2 minutes or just until cooked through. Add the garlic, cabbage, carrot and tomatoes and stir-fry for 1 minute. Add the rice stick noodles and stir-fry for 1 minute. Add the Singapore Sauce and cook for 2 minutes or until well mixed. Add the scallions, cilantro and sesame oil and toss lightly.

Spoon onto serving plates and sprinkle with the fried shallots. Garnish each with a lime wedge.

Many of the ingredients in this recipe, including the fried shallots, can be found in Asian markets.

Serves four

CHEFS' RECIPES

HERB-CRUSTED PRIME RIB WITH PORT WINE SAUCE

Prime Rib

1   (8-pound) 3-rib prime beef rib roast
1   tablespoon chopped fresh parsley
2   teaspoons chopped fresh rosemary
1   teaspoon chopped fresh thyme
2   teaspoons minced garlic
1   teaspoon salt
1   tablespoon coarsely ground pepper

Port Wine Sauce

1   (15-ounce) can beef broth
3/4   cup port
2   tablespoons chopped shallots
1   bay leaf
2   tablespoons flour
3   tablespoons melted butter

To roast the beef, let the prime rib roast stand at room temperature for 2 hours. Combine the parsley, rosemary, thyme, garlic, salt and pepper in a small bowl and mix well. Rub over the surface of the roast. Place the roast fat side up on a rack in a roasting pan; insert a meat thermometer into the center of the roast without touching a rib. Roast at 350 degrees for 2 to 2 1/2 hours or to 120 to 125 degrees on the meat thermometer. Let stand for 15 minutes before carving.

Prepare the sauce during the first hour that the beef is roasting. Combine the beef broth, wine, shallots and bay leaf in a medium saucepan and bring to a boil. Reduce the heat and simmer for 15 to 20 minutes or until of the desired consistency; discard the bay leaf.

Blend the flour and butter in a cup. Add 1/4 of the mixture to the sauce and cook until slightly thickened, stirring constantly; sauce should be thin enough to drizzle. Add more of the butter and flour mixture to the sauce if needed for the desired consistency. Serve with the roast.

Serves six

TEXAS WINE RECOMMENDATION: FLAT CREEK WINERY TRAVIS PEAK CABERNET SAUVIGNON

OVEN-ROASTED BEEF BRISKET

2	tablespoons chili powder
1	tablespoon garlic powder
1	tablespoon onion powder
1	tablespoon sugar
2	teaspoons dry mustard
1	bay leaf, crushed
2	tablespoons salt
1	tablespoon pepper
1	(4-pound) beef brisket
1 1/2	cups beef stock

Combine the chili powder, garlic powder, onion powder, sugar, dry mustard, bay leaf, salt and pepper in a bowl. Rub the mixture over both sides of the brisket. Place in a roasting pan and roast, uncovered, at 350 degrees for 1 hour.

Add the beef stock and enough water to reach 1/2 inch up the side of the roasting pan. Reduce the oven temperature to 300 degrees. Cover the roasting pan tightly with heavy foil and roast for 3 hours longer or until fork-tender.

Trim the fat from the brisket and slice thinly across the grain. Serve with the pan juices.
Serves ten

BARBECUE SAUCE *is a delicious accompaniment for brisket. Mix 2 (32-ounce) bottles of ketchup, 1/4 cup liquid smoke, and 1/4 cup Worcestershire sauce in a large bowl. Rinse the ketchup bottles with 1/2 (12-ounce) can cola and add the cola to the sauce. Add 1 3/4 cups packed brown sugar and 1 ounce pepper and mix until the brown sugar has dissolved. Cook until smooth, stirring frequently. Store the sauce in the emptied ketchup bottles in the refrigerator.*

BEEF TENDERLOIN WITH BORDELAISE SAUCE

Tenderloin

1	(4-pound) beef tenderloin, at room temperature
	Worcestershire sauce
3	garlic cloves, slivered
	bacon slices

Bordelaise Sauce

1/4	cup (1/2 stick) butter
2	shallots, chopped
2	garlic cloves, chopped
2	slices onion
1/2	carrot, chopped
2	sprigs parsley
2	whole cloves
1	bay leaf
10	whole peppercorns
1 1/2	tablespoons flour
1	(10-ounce) can beef bouillon
1	beef bouillon cube
1	cup burgundy
2	tablespoons chopped parsley
1/2	teaspoon salt
1/8	teaspoon pepper

To prepare the tenderloin, rub generously with Worcestershire sauce and place in a roasting pan. Top with the garlic slivers and bacon. Roast at 400 degrees for 40 minutes for rare.

To prepare the sauce, melt the butter in a medium skillet and add the shallots, garlic, onion, carrot, 2 sprigs parsley, cloves, bay leaf and peppercorns. Sauté for 3 minutes or until the onion is golden brown. Remove from the heat and stir in the flour.

Cook over very low heat for 5 minutes or until the flour is light brown, stirring constantly. Remove from the heat and stir in the bouillon, bouillon cube and 3/4 of the wine. Bring just to a boil over medium heat, stirring constantly. Reduce the heat and simmer, uncovered, for 10 minutes, stirring occasionally. Strain the sauce, discarding the vegetables and seasonings. Return to the skillet and add the remaining wine, chopped parsley, salt and pepper. Cook over low heat just until heated through and serve with the beef.
Serves eight

NEED AN EASY MARINADE *for meat? Combine 1/2 cup soy sauce, 1/2 cup vegetable oil, 3 tablespoons sugar, 5 tablespoons brown sugar, 2 tablespoons vinegar, 2 tablespoons ground ginger, and 2 tablespoons garlic powder in a saucepan. Bring to a boil, stirring constantly to blend well. Pour over the steaks and marinate in the refrigerator for 3 to 6 hours. Grill as desired.*

BEEF TENDERLOIN WITH ROQUEFORT PEPPERCORN SAUCE

1	(3- to 4-pound) beef tenderloin, trimmed
3	tablespoons unsalted butter, melted
1	medium shallot, finely chopped
1	tablespoon vegetable oil
2	medium garlic cloves, minced
1/4	cup green peppercorns, rinsed and crushed
1	cup tawny port
2/3	cup heavy cream
2/3	cup (about 3 ounces) crumbled Roquefort cheese
4	teaspoons finely chopped parsley

Tuck under the narrow end of the beef tenderloin to make a roast of uniform thickness and tie lengthwise and crosswise with kitchen twine. Combine the butter and shallot in a bowl and rub over the beef. Place on a rack in a roasting pan and insert a meat thermometer into the thickest portion. Roast at 425 degrees for 45 to 50 minutes or to 130 degrees on the meat thermometer for rare, to 140 degrees for medium-rare or to 160 degrees for well done. Let rest for 10 minutes before carving.

Heat the vegetable oil in a small saucepan. Add the garlic and sauté for 1 minute. Add the green peppercorns and wine and boil over high heat until the mixture is reduced to 1/2 cup. Stir in the cream and cook until reduced by half. Whisk in the Roquefort cheese and heat until the cheese melts and the sauce thickens. Spoon onto serving plates.

Slice the beef and place in the sauce to serve. Garnish with the parsley.
Serves four to six

TEXAS WINE RECOMMENDATION: MESSINA HOF WINERY ZINFANDEL

STUFFED BEEF TENDERLOIN

1/4	cup (1/2 stick) butter, melted
	Worcestershire sauce, fresh lemon juice and cracked pepper to taste
1	(7-pound) beef tenderloin
3	green onions, chopped
1	pound fresh mushrooms, sliced
3/4	cup (1 1/2 sticks) butter
2	cups (8 ounces) crumbled blue or Gorgonzola cheese

Combine 1/4 cup butter with Worcestershire sauce, lemon juice and cracked pepper in a shallow dish and mix well. Add the beef tenderloin and marinate at room temperature for 4 to 5 hours, turning occasionally to marinate evenly.

Sauté the green onions and mushrooms in 3/4 cup butter in a skillet until tender; drain. Remove the tenderloin from the marinade and cut a deep lengthwise slit to form a pocket. Stuff with the cheese and mushroom mixture and close the slit with skewers or kitchen twine. Insert a meat thermometer into the thickest portion of the beef.

Sear the tenderloin on 1 side over very hot coals and turn. Grill to 130 to 140 degrees on the meat thermometer.
Serves eight to ten

TEXAS WINE RECOMMENDATION: BLUE MOUNTAIN VINEYARD CABERNET SAUVIGNON

Mantiquilla de Pobre

4	tomatoes, finely chopped
4	avocados, coarsely chopped
1¹/2	to 2 bunches green onions, thinly sliced
2	tablespoons chopped cilantro
1¹/2	teaspoons salt
2	tablespoons cider vinegar
2	tablespoons vegetable oil
¹/3	cup red wine

Salpicon

8	pounds top sirloin roast or eye of round roast
1	(12-ounce) can diced tomatoes
¹/4	cup chopped cilantro
2	garlic cloves
1	bay leaf
	salt and pepper to taste
2	cups Italian salad dressing
1	cup cooked garbanzo beans (optional)
2	cups (8 ounces) ¹/2-inch cubes Monterey Jack cheese
1	cup chopped green chiles
2	avocados, sliced
1	bunch parsley
	warm tortillas

To prepare the mantiquilla, combine the tomatoes, avocados, green onions and cilantro in a bowl. Season with the salt. Add the vinegar, vegetable oil and wine and mix gently. Chill for 1 hour or longer.

To prepare the salpicon, combine the roast with the tomatoes, cilantro, garlic, bay leaf, salt and pepper in a large heavy saucepan. Add enough water to cover the roast. Cook over medium heat for 5 hours. Drain and cool the beef; cut into 2-inch pieces. Shred the beef into a 9×11-inch dish and add the salad dressing. Marinate in the refrigerator for 8 hours or longer.

To serve, layer the beans, Monterey Jack cheese, green chiles and avocados over the beef. Garnish with the parsley. Serve with warm tortillas in which to roll the beef mixture. Serve with the Mantiquilla de Pobre.

You may also serve the Mantiquilla de Pobre as a dip with chips.

Serves twelve to sixteen

TEXAS WINE RECOMMENDATION: BRUSHY CREEK VINEYARDS AUTUMN SUNSET

LONDON BROIL WITH MUSTARD MARINADE

3	tablespoons each soy sauce and dry white wine
1	tablespoon vegetable oil
1/2	teaspoon Tabasco sauce
1/2	cup Dijon mustard
2	tablespoons brown sugar
1	garlic clove, minced
1	(2-pound) London broil
12	to 15 mushrooms, sliced (optional)

Combine the soy sauce, white wine, vegetable oil and Tabasco sauce in a sealable plastic bag. Add the Dijon mustard, brown sugar and garlic and mix well. Add the beef, turning to coat well. Marinate in the refrigerator for 5 to 24 hours. Drain, reserving the marinade. Grill the beef over hot coals for 5 to 7 minutes on each side, basting frequently with the reserved marinade. Remove to a cutting board and cover loosely with foil; let stand for 5 to 10 minutes. Slice on the diagonal. Combine the reserved marinade with the mushrooms in a saucepan and cook until heated through. Serve with the beef.
Serves six

COWBOY COFFEE STEAK

1/2	cup finely ground coffee
1/4	cup packed brown sugar
1/4	cup kosher salt
1/2	cup coarsely ground pepper
4	(12- to 14-ounce) rib eye steaks
2	tablespoons vegetable oil

Mix the ground coffee, brown sugar, kosher salt and pepper in a small bowl. Press evenly over both sides of the steaks. Heat the vegetable oil until smoking in a skillet large enough to hold the steaks without crowding. Add the steaks and sear for 2 to 3 minutes on each side. Remove to a baking sheet.

Roast the steaks at 450 degrees for 5 to 10 minutes for medium-rare, or until done to taste. Let stand at room temperature for 5 minutes or longer before serving.
Serves four

TEXAS WINE RECOMMENDATION: LA BODEGA WINERY CABERNET SAUVIGNON

VERMOUTH MARINADE *will make meat more flavorful and tender.*

Combine 1 cup vermouth with 1 cup vegetable oil, 1 tablespoon prepared mustard, 2 teaspoons dry mustard, 5 minced garlic cloves, 3 tablespoons Worcestershire sauce, 2 teaspoons salt, and 1 teaspoon pepper in a food processor. Process until the mixture is smooth. Marinate beef in the mixture in the refrigerator for 8 hours or longer and grill as desired.

INDIVIDUAL BEEF WELLINGTONS

6   (1-inch) filets mignons
       seasoned salt and pepper to taste
       vegetable oil
2   tablespoons butter
2   tablespoons minced shallots
8   ounces mushrooms, finely chopped
1/2   teaspoon salt
       pepper to taste
1   (3-ounce) can liver pâté
1   tablespoon brandy
1 1/2 (10-ounce) packages frozen patty shells, thawed
1   egg, lightly beaten

Season the steaks on both sides with the seasoned salt and pepper and brush with vegetable oil. Heat a skillet until very hot. Add the steaks and sear quickly on both sides. Remove to a plate and chill in the refrigerator. Melt the butter in the same skillet and add the shallots. Sauté for 2 minutes. Add the mushrooms, 1/2 teaspoon salt and pepper to taste. Cook for 7 to 8 minutes or until most of the moisture has evaporated. Stir in the liver pâté and brandy. Spread the mixture over the tops of the steaks and return to the refrigerator until chilled.

Press the patty shells into a ball and divide into 12 portions. Roll half the portions into very thin circles on a floured surface. Place each steak on 1 of the circles. Roll the remaining portions of dough into slightly larger circles on the floured surface. Place over the steaks and press the edges to seal; trim away excess dough. Brush the pastry with the egg.

Place the beef on a baking sheet. Bake at 450 degrees for 14 to 16 minutes for rare, for 17 to 19 minutes for medium and for 20 to 22 minutes for well done. Serve immediately.
Serves six

SAVORY BARBECUED RIBS

3/4   cup water
6   tablespoons canola oil
8   teaspoons each cider vinegar and Dijon mustard
8   teaspoons chopped fresh basil
6   garlic cloves, minced
2   teaspoons crushed red pepper
1/2   teaspoon black pepper
2   (8-rib) racks of beef ribs
1   (8-ounce) can tomato sauce

Combine the water, canola oil, vinegar, Dijon mustard, basil, garlic, crushed red pepper and black pepper in a bowl and mix well for the marinade. Pour half the marinade into a sealable plastic bag. Store the remaining marinade in the refrigerator. Cut the rib sections into halves and combine with the marinade in the plastic bag. Marinate in the refrigerator for 1 to 5 days.

Drain the ribs and discard the marinade in the bag. Place the ribs in a shallow roasting pan. Add the tomato sauce to the unused marinade and mix well. Pour over the ribs. Roast at 350 degrees for 1 hour. Grill over hot coals for 30 minutes longer.

You may omit the grilling step if preferred and roast the ribs for a total of 1 1/2 hours.
Serves four

TEXAS WINE RECOMMENDATION: PILLAR BLUFF VINEYARDS WHITE MERLOT

BEEF FILETS WITH WINE SAUCE

6   (1- to 1¹/2-inch) beef tenderloin steaks
¹/2   teaspoon salt
1   teaspoon freshly ground pepper
2   tablespoons olive oil
1   (10-ounce) can beef broth
1   cup dry red wine
2   garlic cloves, minced
3   tablespoons green peppercorns
¹/4   cup (¹/2 stick) unsalted butter, sliced

Sprinkle the steaks evenly with the salt and pepper. Heat a 5-quart sauté pan over high heat and add the olive oil. Add the steaks and sear until brown on both sides. Remove the steaks from the sauté pan and add the beef broth, wine and garlic, stirring to deglaze the pan. Return the steaks to the pan and cook for 3 to 5 minutes on each side or until done to taste.

Remove from the heat and transfer the steaks to a platter, reserving the sauce in the pan. Add the peppercorns to the pan and whisk in the butter gradually. Serve over the steaks.
Serves six

TEXAS WINE RECOMMENDATION: DELANEY VALLEY CLARET

TEXAS IS KNOWN *as the livestock capital of the world and is the top producer of the nation's beef cattle. Although Plano is no longer the ranching community of years past, you don't have to look far to find its true roots. The Haggards, one of Plano's founding families, still own and operate a farm where longhorns graze the pastures right in the middle of town. Collin County is also home to Southfork, the world's most famous ranch. Before it was known as the home of the Ewing Oil tycoons on the television show "Dallas," Southfork Ranch was an active working ranch. Fame, fortune, and a flood of tourists led them to hang up their spurs and bow out of the cattle business in the 1980s.*

SOUTHWEST CHIMAYO CHILE BURGERS

Chipotle Mayonnaise

2	canned chipotle peppers in adobo sauce
1	egg yolk
1	tablespoon sherry vinegar
1	tablespoon prepared mustard
	juice of 1/2 lemon
	salt to taste
1	cup vegetable oil

Burgers

4	Anaheim peppers
31/2	pounds ground beef
2	teaspoons chili powder
	salt and pepper to taste
2	tablespoons olive oil
2	cups (8 ounces) shredded Monterey Jack cheese with jalapeño peppers
8	sandwich buns
	sliced tomato
	sliced red onion
	sliced avocado

To prepare the mayonnaise, combine the peppers, egg yolk, vinegar, mustard, lemon juice and salt in a food processor and process until smooth. Add the vegetable oil very gradually, processing constantly until thickened and smooth.

To prepare the burgers, roast the peppers over hot coals or broil until the skins are blackened. Cool and peel the peppers. Split the peppers lengthwise, discarding the seeds.

Divide the ground beef into 16 portions, and shape into patties. Season with the chili powder, salt and pepper; brush with the olive oil. Place a pepper half on 8 of the patties and top each with 1/4 cup of the shredded cheese. Top with the remaining patties and press the edges firmly to seal.

Grill the burgers until done to taste. Serve on the buns with the mayonnaise and garnish with the tomato, red onion and avocado.

To avoid uncooked eggs that may carry salmonella, you can use an equivalent amount of pasteurized egg substitute.

Serves eight

MARGARITAS *have long been served around the world, but the origin of the popular drink is clouded in mystery. One of the most famous claims involves Dallas socialite Margarita Sames. In 1948 she hosted a Christmas pool party at her vacation home in Acapulco. That evening she concocted various cocktails, one of which included mixing three parts of tequila with one part Cointreau and one part lime juice. The resulting cocktail became a grand success among Texans and quickly caught on under the name of its creator.*

CROWN ROAST OF PORK WITH
CRANBERRY SAUSAGE STUFFING

1   (10-pound) 16-rib crown pork roast
1/8   teaspoon salt
1/2   teaspoon pepper
8   ounces bulk pork sausage
1   (8-ounce) package herb-seasoned stuffing mix
1   (16-ounce) can whole cranberry sauce
1 1/2   cups chopped cooking apples
1/4   cup (1/2 stick) butter or margarine, melted

Season the roast with salt and pepper. Place bone ends up on a rack in a shallow roasting pan. Insert a meat thermometer into the thickest portion of the roast, taking care not to touch a bone.

Brown the sausage in a skillet, stirring until crumbly; drain. Add the stuffing mix, cranberry sauce, apples and butter and mix well. Spoon into the center of the roast and cover the stuffing and the ends of the bones with foil. Roast at 325 degrees for 4 hours or to 160 degrees on the meat thermometer.

Serves ten to twelve

TEXAS WINE RECOMMENDATION: MESSINA HOF WINERY JOHANNESBURG RIESLING

APRICOT AND CRANBERRY-STUFFED
PORK LOIN

1   cup water
3/4   cup chopped dried apricots
1/2   cup dried cranberries
2   tablespoons butter
1   (6-ounce) package chicken-flavor stuffing mix
1   tablespoon fresh lemon juice
1/3   cup chopped pecans
1   (3-pound) pork loin roast
3/4   teaspoon salt
1/2   teaspoon pepper

Bring the water to a boil in a 2-quart saucepan and add the apricots, cranberries and butter. Simmer, covered, for 5 minutes. Add the stuffing mix, lemon juice and pecans and mix well. Let stand, covered, for 5 minutes.

Butterfly the pork loin and lay flat on a work surface. Spread the stuffing mixture over the pork and roll the pork from the narrow end to enclose the filling; secure with kitchen twine. Season with the salt and pepper.

Place in a roasting pan and insert a meat thermometer into the thickest portion of the pork. Roast at 350 degrees for 1 1/2 hours or to 150 degrees on the meat thermometer. Let stand for 10 minutes. Remove the kitchen twine and carve to serve.

Serves eight

CHORIZO-STUFFED PORK TENDERLOIN

Pork Tenderloin

8   ounces ground chorizo, cooked, drained and cooled
1   cup shredded Monterey Jack cheese
1/2 cup sliced white onion
2   poblano peppers, roasted and peeled
1   (1 1/2-pound) pork tenderloin
3   tablespoons vegetable oil

Roasted Garlic Cream Sauce

4   cups (1 quart) heavy cream
4   ounces ground chorizo, cooked and drained
1/2 cup roasted garlic

To prepare the pork, combine the chorizo with the Monterey Jack cheese and onion in a bowl and mix well. Spoon the mixture into the poblano peppers.

Butterfly the pork tenderloin and lay flat on a work surface. Pound 1/8 inch thick. Arrange the stuffed peppers on the pork and close the pork to enclose the peppers; secure with kitchen twine. Insert a meat thermometer into the thickest portion of the pork.

Heat 1 tablespoon of the vegetable oil in a large ovenproof skillet. Add the tenderloin and sear until brown on all sides. Place the skillet in a 350-degree oven and roast the pork for 10 to 15 minutes or to 145 to 150 degrees on the meat thermometer. Cool to room temperature and chill in the refrigerator.

Slice the pork into 1/2- to 3/4-inch medallions. Heat 2 tablespoons vegetable oil in a skillet and add the medallions. Cook until seared on both sides. Remove to a serving plate and keep warm.

To prepare the sauce, heat the cream in a medium saucepan over medium heat. Cook until reduced by half. Stir in the chorizo and garlic. Cook just until heated through; do not boil. Serve immediately with the pork.

To get 1/2 cup of roasted garlic, roast about 2 heads of garlic for 20 minutes.

Serves four to six

TO **BUTTERFLY** *a pork tenderloin easily, cut along its length with a sharp knife, cutting to within 1/2 inch of the bottom. Press the tenderloin open to lie flat. This increases the surface area into which a marinade can penetrate or affords the opportunity to stuff the center with a filling. The halves can be folded back over the filling and the sides secured with skewers or tied with kitchen twine.*

ROASTED PORK TENDERLOIN WITH BRANDIED MUSHROOMS

Pork Tenderloin

1	(1 1/2- to 2-pound) pork tenderloin
1	tablespoon Dijon mustard
1	teaspoon salt, or to taste
1/2	teaspoon pepper, or to taste
1	tablespoon olive oil
1	teaspoon rosemary
1/4	cup beef stock

Brandied Mushrooms

	reserved cooking juices
2	cups sliced fresh mushrooms
	olive oil
1	cup beef stock
2	tablespoons brandy or Cognac
2	teaspoons cornstarch
2	to 3 teaspoons water
	salt and pepper to taste

To prepare the tenderloin, rub it on all sides with the Dijon mustard, salt and pepper, coating well. Heat the olive oil in a large ovenproof skillet over medium-high heat. Add the tenderloin and brown on all sides. Mix the rosemary and beef stock in a cup and add to the skillet. Place the skillet in a 350-degree oven and roast for 30 to 40 minutes or until the pork is cooked through. Remove to a serving platter and cover with foil to keep warm; reserve the cooking juices in the skillet.

To prepare the mushrooms, place the skillet over medium heat and cook until most of the reserved liquid evaporates. Add the mushrooms and a small amount of olive oil if needed. Sauté until the mushrooms are golden brown. Add the beef stock, stirring to deglaze the skillet. Cook over high heat until the liquid is reduced to about 3/4 cup. Stir in the brandy and cook for 1 to 2 minutes or until the alcohol evaporates. Remove from the heat.

Dissolve the cornstarch in the water in a small bowl. Add to the sauce and cook over low heat just until the mixture thickens, stirring constantly. Season with salt and pepper.

Cut the tenderloin into thin slices and serve with the brandied mushrooms.

Serves four to six

TEXAS WINE RECOMMENDATION: CROSS ROADS CABERNET FRANC

PORK MEDALLIONS WITH APPLES AND CIDER CREAM SAUCE

Pork and Apples

1   (1 1/2-pound) pork tenderloin
     salt and pepper to taste
2   tablespoons butter
3   Granny Smith apples, peeled and cut into 10 slices each
1   tablespoon butter

Cider Cream Sauce

1   shallot, finely chopped
1   tablespoon butter
1   cup apple cider or apple juice
1/2   cup cider vinegar
1/2   teaspoon sage
1   cup chicken broth
1 1/2   cups cream

To prepare the pork and apples, cut the tenderloin into 1-inch slices and flatten to 1/2 inch with a meat mallet. Season with salt and pepper. Sauté in 2 tablespoons butter in a skillet over medium heat for 4 minutes or just until cooked through. Remove to a plate and cover to keep warm.

Sauté the apple slices in 1 tablespoon butter in a skillet just until tender. Remove to the plate with the pork and cover to keep warm.

To prepare the sauce, sauté the shallot in the butter in the same skillet. Add the apple cider, cider vinegar and sage and cook until reduced by half. Stir in the chicken broth and cook until reduced by half. Stir in the cream.

Return the pork and apples to the skillet and cook for 1 minute or until heated through. Serve over rice.

Serves six

REFRESH YOUR GUESTS *after a messy meal or before a buffet. Set out a platter of rolled washcloths that have been dampened and frozen. You can add lemon juice or an essential oil to the water if you like. Also remember to have a dish handy for the used cloths. Your guests will love this special touch.*

HONEY SESAME PORK TENDERLOIN

1/2   cup soy sauce
1   tablespoon sesame oil
2   garlic cloves, minced
1   tablespoon grated gingerroot
1   (1-pound) pork tenderloin
1/4   cup honey
2   tablespoons brown sugar
1/4   cup sesame seeds

Combine the soy sauce, sesame oil, garlic and gingerroot in a sealable plastic bag. Add the tenderloin and seal the bag, turning to coat evenly. Marinate in the refrigerator for 2 hours or longer. Drain the pork and pat dry with paper towels. Mix the honey and brown sugar on a plate. Spread the sesame seeds on a plate or waxed paper. Roll the pork in the honey mixture and then in the sesame seeds, coating evenly. Place the pork in a shallow roasting pan lined with foil; insert a meat thermometer into the thickest portion of the meat. Roast at 375 degrees for 25 to 30 minutes or to 160 degrees on the meat thermometer. Slice and serve.

Serves six

SPICY BABY BACK RIBS

1/4   cup paprika
2   teaspoons onion powder
2   teaspoons garlic powder
2   teaspoons salt
2   teaspoons white pepper
1   teaspoon ground red pepper
2   teaspoons black pepper
4   to 6 pounds pork loin baby back ribs or pork spareribs
        barbecue sauce

Mix the paprika, onion powder, garlic powder, salt, white pepper, red pepper and black pepper in a bowl. Rub the mixture over the ribs, coating evenly.

Heat the coals in a grill and arrange the coals in a circle or on the sides, leaving the center open. Place the ribs in the center of the grill. Grill, covered, for 5 to 6 hours or until very tender, turning every 30 minutes and adding coals as needed to maintain the grilling temperature. Brush the ribs with barbecue sauce and grill for 20 minutes longer, turning and brushing again with the sauce after 10 minutes.

Serves four to six

PROSCIUTTO AND
PROVOLONE-STUFFED FOCACCIA

1   envelope dry yeast
1¹/2   cups lukewarm milk
1   cup semolina flour
¹/4   cup olive oil
¹/2   teaspoon salt
3¹/4   cups bread flour
4   ounces thinly sliced provolone cheese
4   ounces thinly sliced prosciutto
¹/4   cup minced fresh chives

Sprinkle the yeast over the lukewarm milk in a bowl and let stand for 5 minutes. Add the semolina flour, olive oil, salt and 3 cups of the bread flour and mix to form a stiff dough. Knead on a floured surface for 10 minutes, kneading in enough of the remaining ¹/4 cup bread flour to prevent sticking.

Place the dough in a large greased bowl, turning to coat the surface. Let rise for 45 minutes or until doubled in bulk. Punch down the dough and let rest for 5 minutes. Roll to a 10×15-inch rectangle on a lightly floured surface.

Arrange half the provolone cheese crosswise down the center of the dough. Top with half the prosciutto and half the chives. Fold 1 end of the dough over the filling and arrange the remaining cheese, prosciutto and chives on the fold. Fold the remaining end of the dough over the filling and press lightly; press the ends to seal.

Place on a large baking sheet sprayed with nonstick cooking spray. Cover with a damp towel and let rise for 45 minutes or until doubled in bulk. Bake at 375 degrees for 20 minutes or until golden brown. Cool on a rack for 10 minutes. Slice diagonally and serve warm.
Serves ten

CUMBERLAND EASTER HAM

1   (7- to 10-pound) fully cooked spiral-sliced ham
8   to 10 fresh rosemary sprigs
1   tablespoon butter
1/4   cup minced onion
1   (12-ounce) jar currant jelly
1   tablespoon grated orange zest
1/4   cup orange juice
1   tablespoon grated lemon zest
1/4   cup lemon juice
1   tablespoon Dijon mustard
1   cup port
      rosemary sprigs, orange slices and/or lemon slices

Unwrap the ham and remove the plastic disk covering the bone. Place the 8 to 10 rosemary sprigs between every 2 or 3 slices of ham. Place the ham cut side down in an oven-cooking bag.

Melt the butter in a saucepan over medium heat. Add the onion and sauté until tender. Stir in the currant jelly, orange zest, orange juice, lemon zest, lemon juice and Dijon mustard. Cook over medium heat until the jelly melts, stirring to mix well. Add the wine and simmer for 5 to 10 minutes or until of the desired consistency.

Add the jelly mixture to the cooking bag and seal the bag. Cut three 1/2-inch slits in the top of the bag and place in a baking pan. Place on the lowest oven rack. Bake at 275 degrees for 2 1/2 hours. Let stand in the cooking bag for 15 minutes.

Remove the ham to a carving board. Separate the slices and arrange on a serving platter. Spoon the cooking sauce over the slices. Garnish with additional rosemary sprigs, orange slices and/or lemon slices.
Serves ten to twelve

TEXAS WINE RECOMMENDATION: DRIFTWOOD VINEYARDS VIOGNIER

MUSTARD SAUCE *is a savory addition to baked ham. Beat 8 egg yolks in a bowl and stir in 1/4 cup sugar, 1/4 cup vinegar, 1/2 cup prepared mustard, 2 tablespoons dry mustard, and 1 teaspoon salt. Spoon into a double boiler and cook over low heat until thickened, stirring constantly. Cool completely and stir in 2 cups heavy cream and 4 chopped hard-cooked eggs. Adjust the seasoning and serve warm.*

RACK OF LAMB WITH
ROSEMARY SCALLION CRUST

1¹/₂   tablespoons olive oil
¹/₄   teaspoon dried hot red pepper flakes
1   garlic clove, minced
3   tablespoons sliced scallion bulb and green portion
1   tablespoon chopped fresh rosemary, or 1 teaspoon dried rosemary
¹/₂   cup fresh bread crumbs
   salt and black pepper to taste
1   (1¹/₄-pound) 7- or 8-rib Frenched single rack of lamb

Heat the olive oil in a small skillet over medium heat until hot but not smoking. Add the red pepper flakes and sauté for 10 seconds. Add the garlic and sauté for 30 seconds. Add the scallion and rosemary and sauté for 10 seconds. Stir in the bread crumbs and season with salt and black pepper. Remove from the heat.

Season the lamb with salt and black pepper. Heat an ovenproof skillet over medium-high heat and add the lamb. Brown for 5 minutes, turning to brown the ends and sides evenly. Drain the skillet and arrange the lamb fat side up in the skillet. Pat the crumb mixture evenly over the top of the lamb. Insert a meat thermometer into the thickest portion, taking care that it does not touch a bone.

Place on the center oven rack and roast at 475 degrees for 15 minutes or to 130 degrees on the meat thermometer for medium-rare. Remove to a serving platter and let stand for 10 minutes before serving.

Serves two

TEXAS WINE RECOMMENDATION: LONE OAK VINEYARDS MERLOT

The photograph for this recipe is on page 121.

OSSO BUCO

1	cup flour
	salt and pepper to taste
2¹/2	to 3 pounds veal shanks
1	cup olive oil
1	cup dry red wine
1	onion, chopped
1	rib celery, chopped
1	garlic clove, finely chopped
1	bouquet garni of thyme, rosemary, sage and bay leaf (see below)
3	cups marinara sauce
3	cups beef stock

Mix the flour with salt and pepper on waxed paper. Coat the veal shanks with the flour mixture. Heat a heavy roasting pan over high heat on the stove top. Add the olive oil and heat until hot. Add the veal shanks and brown on all sides. Remove the veal shanks from the pan.

Add the wine to the drippings in the pan, stirring to deglaze the pan. Stir in the onion, celery, garlic and bouquet garni. Season with salt and pepper. Return the veal shanks to the pan. Roast, uncovered, at 500 degrees for 10 minutes.

Stir in the marinara sauce and beef stock. Reduce the oven temperature to 200 degrees. Roast, covered, for 1 hour or until tender. Serve with risotto, noodles or mashed potatoes.
Serves six to eight

A BOUQUET GARNI *typically includes parsley, thyme, rosemary, sage, and bay leaves. Chop the herbs coarsely in a food processor or by hand and tie in a cheesecloth bag. Include when cooking soups, stews, braised dishes, and sauces. You can also make a garni of cinnamon, cloves, mint leaves, or other favorite spices to flavor cider or wine for a delicious warm drink.*

FLOWERPOT CHICKEN PIE

Pastry

3	cups flour
3	tablespoons sugar
1	teaspoon salt
1	cup (2 sticks) unsalted butter, chilled and cut into pieces
2	egg yolks, lightly beaten
1/4	cup (about) ice water

Filling

1	chicken
1	bay leaf
1	garlic clove, minced
4	cups water or chicken stock
3	cups thinly sliced carrots
2	cups chopped peeled potatoes
1	cup finely chopped onion
1/2	cup sherry
2	cups green peas
1	cup sliced mushrooms
1	tablespoon finely chopped fresh basil
1/2	cup (1 stick) butter
1/2	cup flour
2	cups heavy cream
	salt and freshly ground pepper to taste
3	egg yolks, beaten

To prepare the pastry, mix the flour, sugar and salt in a medium bowl. Cut in the butter with a pastry blender or 2 knives until the mixture is crumbly. Add the egg yolks. Add water 1 tablespoon at a time, mixing until the dough sticks together.

Divide into 2 portions and shape into balls. Flatten into disks, wrap in plastic wrap and chill for 30 minutes to 8 hours. Roll each portion 1/8 inch thick on a floured surface. Cut each portion into six 6-inch circles. Cover with plastic wrap.

To prepare the filling, combine the chicken with the bay leaf, garlic and water in a large stockpot and cook until the chicken is tender. Remove the chicken, reserving the cooking liquid. Cool and cut up the chicken, discarding the skin and bones.

Add the carrots, potatoes, onion and sherry to the reserved cooking liquid. Cook over medium heat until the vegetables are tender. Add the peas, mushrooms and basil. Cook for 8 minutes longer. Discard the bay leaf.

Melt the butter in a medium saucepan and stir in the flour. Cook until bubbly. Add the cream gradually and cook until thickened and smooth, stirring constantly. Add the chicken and vegetables with the cooking liquid. Simmer until thickened to the desired consistency, stirring frequently. Season with salt and pepper.

Spoon into 12 terra cotta flowerpots or baking ramekins. Top each with a pastry circle and brush with the beaten egg yolks. Bake at 350 degrees until the filling is bubbly and the crust is golden brown.

You may also prepare as a double-crust 8-inch pie if preferred.

Serves twelve

TEXAS WINE RECOMMENDATION: PHEASANT RIDGE WINERY CHARDONNAY

CARIBBEAN CHICKEN SKEWERS WITH MANGO SALSA

Chicken

1/2	small red onion
4	green onions
2	garlic cloves
1/2	jalapeño pepper, seeded
2	tablespoons soy sauce
1/4	cup vegetable oil
1	teaspoon each allspice and ground cinnamon
1/4	teaspoon freshly grated nutmeg
1 1/2	teaspoons salt
1	teaspoon freshly ground pepper
1	pound boneless skinless chicken breasts

Mango Salsa

1	mango, peeled and chopped
1/2	jalapeño pepper, seeded and finely chopped
1/2	small red onion, finely chopped
2	tablespoons chopped cilantro
1	teaspoon sugar
	grated zest of 1/2 lime
	juice of 1 lime

To prepare the chicken, combine the red onion, green onions, garlic, jalapeño pepper, soy sauce and vegetable oil in a food processor. Add the allspice, cinnamon, nutmeg, salt and pepper and process to form a thick paste. Cut the chicken into strips and combine with the paste in a bowl, coating well. Marinate in the refrigerator for 8 hours or longer.

Thread the chicken onto skewers. Grill over hot coals or on a grill surface for 3 minutes on each side or until cooked through.

To prepare the salsa, combine the mango, jalapeño pepper, onion and cilantro in a bowl. Add the sugar, lime zest and lime juice and toss lightly to mix. Serve the chicken warm or at room temperature with the salsa.

You may prepare the salsa up to 12 hours in advance, adding the lime juice just before serving. You may substitute Caribbean spice blend for the seasonings in the marinade.
Serves four

ROASTING PEPPERS *is not difficult and the difference in taste is undeniable!*

Arrange the peppers in a single layer on a baking sheet and roast at 450 degrees for 45 minutes or until the skins begin to blister. Remove the peppers to a plastic bag and let stand for 10 to 15 minutes or until they sweat and the skins loosen. Rinse under cool water and discard the skins, seeds, and veins. It is a good idea to wear gloves when handling hot peppers and to avoid touching your eyes after handling the seeds.

BASIL CHICKEN PICCATA

4	boneless skinless chicken breasts
1/4	to 1/2 teaspoon salt
	freshly ground pepper to taste
2	tablespoons olive oil
2	garlic cloves, chopped
2	teaspoons chopped shallots
2	teaspoons grated lemon zest
2	to 3 tablespoons fresh lemon juice
1	tablespoon capers
1/2	cup white wine
1	tablespoon chopped fresh basil
	shaved Parmigiano-Reggiano cheese

Season the chicken with the salt and pepper; pound lightly if necessary to reduce the thickness to 3/4 inch. Heat the olive oil in a skillet. Add the chicken and sear for 2 to 3 minutes or until brown on the bottom. Turn the chicken and add the garlic and shallots. Sauté until the vegetables are light brown.

Add the lemon zest, lemon juice, capers, wine and basil. Cook for 3 to 4 minutes or until the chicken is cooked through and the sauce is reduced by half. Garnish with the cheese.
Serves four

GREEN ENCHILADAS

1	pound fresh spinach, chopped
1	onion, chopped
1/4	cup (1/2 stick) butter
3	cups (24 ounces) sour cream
1	(4-ounce) can chopped green chiles, or 2 fresh green chiles, chopped
1/4	cup milk
1	teaspoon ground cumin
2	pounds boneless skinless chicken breasts, cooked and chopped
12	flour tortillas
1 1/2	cups (6 ounces) shredded Monterey Jack cheese

Cook or steam the spinach in a small amount of water in a saucepan. Drain, reserving 1/2 cup cooking liquid. Sauté the onion in the butter in a saucepan. Add the spinach, the reserved cooking liquid, sour cream, green chiles, milk and cumin and mix well. Remove and reserve half the sauce. Add the chicken to the sauce remaining in the saucepan and mix well.

Heat the tortillas in a 350-degree oven for 3 minutes to soften. Arrange the tortillas on a work surface. Spoon the chicken mixture into the centers of the tortillas and roll to enclose the filling. Place seam side down in a single layer in a lightly buttered baking dish.

Layer half the Monterey Jack cheese, the reserved sauce and the remaining cheese over the rolled tortillas. Bake at 350 degrees for 30 minutes.
Serves six

TEXAS WINE RECOMMENDATION: HAAK VINEYARDS BLANC DU BOIS

SOUR CREAM CHICKEN ENCHILADAS

3	tablespoons butter
1	cup chopped onion
1/4	cup flour
1	teaspoon cumin
3/4	teaspoon salt
2 1/2	cups chicken broth
1	(4-ounce) can chopped green chiles
1	cup (8 ounces) sour cream
1 1/2	cups (6 ounces) shredded Monterey Jack cheese
2	cups chopped cooked chicken
12	(6-inch) flour tortillas

Melt the butter in a skillet. Add the onion and sauté until the onion is translucent. Stir in the flour and cook for 1 to 2 minutes or until bubbly. Stir in the cumin and salt. Add the chicken broth gradually and cook until thickened, stirring constantly. Add the green chiles. Remove from the heat and stir in the sour cream and half the Monterey Jack cheese.

Spoon the chicken onto the tortillas and top each with 1 to 2 tablespoons of the sauce. Roll the tortillas to enclose the filling. Place seam side down in a 9×13-inch baking pan.

Spoon the remaining sauce over the rolled tortillas and top with the remaining 3/4 cup Monterey Jack cheese. Bake at 350 degrees for 25 minutes or until the cheese melts and the sauce is bubbly.

You may substitute 2 additional cups of the cheese for the chicken to prepare meatless cheese enchiladas.

Serves six

TORTILLAS *often need to be softened before use to prevent cracking. Traditionally tortillas were dipped into hot oil for a few seconds on each side. You can also dip them into the warmed sauce from the dish that you are preparing. A healthy alternative is to spray each tortilla lightly with cooking spray or brush it lightly with water; then wrap the tortillas in paper towels and microwave on High for 30 seconds to 2 minutes, depending on the number of tortillas needed.*

GRILLED CHICKEN

4   bone-in chicken breasts
     salt and pepper to taste
     hot cooked rice
     Apple Pico de Gallo (below)

Trim the chicken and sprinkle lightly with salt and pepper. Heat a charcoal, wood or gas grill to medium and place a rack 6 inches from the heat source. Grill the chicken for 20 to 30 minutes or until the chicken is cooked through.

Serve the chicken over rice with Apple Pico de Gallo. You may also serve with the Peach Pico de Gallo or Spicy Pineapple Salsa on page 147.

You may substitute boneless chicken breasts for the bone-in chicken and place the rack closer to the heat source in order to brown the meat without drying out. Grill for just 3 to 4 minutes on each side.
Serves four

APPLE PICO DE GALLO

2   crisp apples, such as Red Delicious, Fuji or Granny Smith, chopped
1/2   red onion, chopped
1   jalapeño pepper, minced
1/2   bunch cilantro, chopped
       juice of 1 lime
       kosher salt to taste

Combine the apples, onion, jalapeño pepper, cilantro and lime juice in a bowl. Season to taste with kosher salt. Chill in the refrigerator until serving time or for up to 24 hours.
Makes two and one-half cups

GRILLED VEGETABLES *are a wonderful addition to that dinner prepared under a starry Texas sky. Just throw the vegetables on the grill along with the meat. Fold a piece of heavy foil in half and crimp the edges together to make a pouch. Place the vegetables in the pouch and season with spices and butter. Fold the top edge of the pouch to seal, allowing enough room for steam to expand the pouch. Grill over medium-hot coals for 20 to 25 minutes or until the vegetables are tender.*

PEACH PICO DE GALLO

4	peaches, coarsely chopped
1	red bell pepper, seeded and chopped
1	large red onion, chopped
1/2	cup chopped cilantro
2	garlic cloves, minced
2	jalapeño peppers, seeded and chopped
1/2	cup pineapple juice
6	tablespoons lime juice
	salt and pepper to taste

Combine the peaches, red bell pepper, onion, cilantro, garlic and jalapeño peppers in a bowl. Add the pineapple juice and lime juice; season with salt and pepper and mix well. Chill in the refrigerator for several hours. Serve with grilled chicken or fish.

Makes six cups

SPICY PINEAPPLE SALSA

1	(8-ounce) can crushed pineapple, drained
1/4	cup chopped cilantro
2	or 3 garlic cloves, minced
2	green onions, chopped
1	jalapeño pepper, seeded and minced
2	tablespoons fresh lime juice
1/2	teaspoon salt

Combine the crushed pineapple, cilantro, garlic, green onions and jalapeño pepper in a bowl. Add the lime juice and salt and mix well. Chill, covered, for 2 hours. Serve with fish or chicken.

Makes one and one-fourth cups

CHICKEN TACOS WITH
HONEY CHIPOTLE SAUCE

Honey Chipotle Sauce

1	ounce canned chipotle peppers in adobo sauce, chopped
1	teaspoon minced garlic
1	teaspoon chopped fresh cilantro (optional)
1/2	cup honey
1/2	cup fresh lime juice
1	tablespoon balsamic vinegar
1/4	cup vegetable oil
1	tablespoon dry mustard
1	teaspoon ground cumin

Tacos

2	pounds boneless skinless chicken breasts, cooked and chopped
8	(6-inch) flour tortillas
	shredded lettuce
	chopped tomatoes
	shredded cheese
	sour cream

To prepare the sauce, combine the chipotle peppers with the garlic and cilantro in a bowl. Add the honey, lime juice, balsamic vinegar, vegetable oil, dry mustard and cumin and mix well.

To prepare the tacos, spoon the chicken onto the tortillas and add the lettuce, tomatoes, cheese and sour cream. Top with the chipotle sauce. Serve immediately.

You may serve the tacos with salsa instead of the Honey Chipotle Sauce if preferred.

Serves four

SAUTÉED CHICKEN BREASTS WITH
ORANGE DIJON SAUCE

Chicken

2	tablespoons butter
1	tablespoon olive oil
4	boneless skinless chicken breasts with the tenderloins removed
	salt and pepper to taste
1/2	cup flour

Orange Dijon Sauce

2/3	cup orange juice
2	teaspoons Dijon mustard
1	tablespoon brown sugar
1	teaspoon minced fresh rosemary
2	tablespoons butter

To prepare the chicken, melt the butter with the olive oil in a 12-inch skillet over medium-low heat. Sprinkle the chicken with salt and pepper and coat with the flour. Increase the heat under the skillet to medium-high and heat until the oil mixture is hot and the butter is golden brown and smells nutty. Add the chicken and cook for 7 minutes, turning once. Remove the chicken to a serving platter.

To prepare the sauce, combine the orange juice, Dijon mustard, brown sugar and rosemary in a bowl and mix well. Add to the skillet, stirring to deglaze the bottom. Cook until the liquid is reduced by half. Tilt the skillet and drain the sauce to one side. Whisk in the butter. Spoon over the chicken to serve.
Serves four

TEXAS WINE RECOMMENDATION: LA BODEGA WINERY CHARDONNAY RESERVE

CHICKEN MARSALA

4	boneless skinless chicken breasts, cut into quarters
1/4	to 1/2 cup olive oil
1 1/2	cups (or more) flour
2	eggs, lightly beaten
1 1/2	cups (or more) Italian bread crumbs
1/2	cup (1 stick) butter
2	cups marsala
1	garlic clove, minced
2	teaspoons dried basil
2	teaspoons Italian seasoning, or 1 teaspoon oregano
1/4	teaspoon white pepper or black pepper
1/4	to 1/2 cup (1/2 to 1 stick) butter
16	ounces fresh mushrooms, sliced

Pound the chicken to a thickness of 1/4 inch. Heat 1/4 cup olive oil in a large skillet. Roll the chicken pieces in the flour, dip into the eggs and then into the bread crumbs, coating evenly. Add to the skillet and sauté until light brown, adding additional olive oil if needed. Remove and drain the chicken.

Melt 1/2 cup butter in a clean skillet. Stir in the wine, garlic, basil, Italian seasoning and white pepper. Cook over medium heat until slightly thickened, stirring constantly. Add 1/4 to 1/2 cup butter gradually, cooking until heated through and of the desired consistency. Add the chicken and mushrooms to the skillet. Simmer for 30 minutes. Serve over angel hair pasta.
Serves six to eight

TEXAS WINE RECOMMENDATION: TEXAS HILLS VINEYARDS SANGIOVESE

CHICKEN WITH PISTACHIO PESTO PASTA

Pistachio Pesto

1	cup (4 ounces) grated fresh Parmesan cheese
1	cup crushed pistachios
1/2	cup olive oil
10	garlic cloves, minced
1	cup packed basil leaves
1/4	cup packed parsley leaves
1/2	teaspoon salt
1/2	teaspoon pepper

Chicken and Pasta

16	ounces uncooked farfalle pasta
1	tablespoon olive oil
2	teaspoons balsamic vinegar
1/2	teaspoon garlic salt
4	boneless skinless chicken breasts, chopped

To prepare the pesto, combine the Parmesan cheese, pistachios, olive oil, garlic, basil, parsley, salt and pepper in a food processor and process to a thick paste. Remove 1/2 cup of the pesto for this recipe; reserve or freeze the remaining pesto for another use.

To prepare the chicken and pasta, cook the farfalle al dente using the package directions. Combine the olive oil, balsamic vinegar and garlic salt in a skillet and mix well. Add the chicken and cook until cooked through.

Drain the pasta and combine with the chicken in a bowl. Add the pesto and toss to coat well. Serve immediately.

Serves four to six

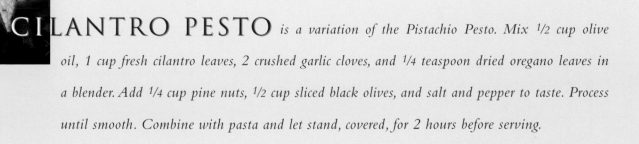

CILANTRO PESTO *is a variation of the Pistachio Pesto. Mix 1/2 cup olive oil, 1 cup fresh cilantro leaves, 2 crushed garlic cloves, and 1/4 teaspoon dried oregano leaves in a blender. Add 1/4 cup pine nuts, 1/2 cup sliced black olives, and salt and pepper to taste. Process until smooth. Combine with pasta and let stand, covered, for 2 hours before serving.*

THAI TURKEY ROLL-UPS

Peanut Mayonnaise

1	tablespoon peanut butter
2	tablespoons lime juice
2	tablespoons mayonnaise
1	garlic clove, crushed
1/2	teaspoon ground ginger
1/8	teaspoon (or more) ground or flaked red pepper

Roll-Ups

4	(10-inch) flour tortillas
1/2	cup chopped fresh basil
4	large green cabbage leaves
8	thin slices cooked turkey, about 8 to 10 ounces
1	cup red bell pepper slices

To prepare the mayonnaise, combine the peanut butter, lime juice, mayonnaise, garlic, ginger and red pepper in a bowl and mix well.

To prepare the roll-ups, spread the mayonnaise on the tortillas. Top each with 2 tablespoons basil, 1 cabbage leaf, 2 slices turkey and 1/4 cup red bell pepper. Roll the tortillas to enclose the filling. Wrap each tortilla in plastic wrap and chill until serving time.
Serves four

GRILLED MAHI MAHI WITH RED PEPPER CREAM AND TOMATILLO AND CORN SALSA

Tomatillo and Corn Salsa

10	medium tomatillos
2	Anaheim peppers
1	ear fresh corn, or 1/2 cup frozen corn kernels, thawed
2	garlic cloves, minced
3	tablespoons chopped basil
2	tablespoons olive oil
1	tablespoon sherry vinegar
	salt and pepper to taste

Red Pepper Cream

2	red bell peppers, seeded and coarsely chopped
2	garlic cloves, minced
1	shallot, minced
1/2	cup white wine
1/4	cup white wine vinegar
1	cup heavy cream
1/2	cup (1 stick) unsalted butter, chopped
	salt and white pepper to taste

Mahi Mahi

1 1/2	pounds mahi mahi, cut into 6 portions
1/4	cup olive oil
	salt and pepper to taste

To prepare the salsa, blanch the tomatillos in boiling water; discard the husks and chop the tomatillos. Split the peppers into halves and chop, discarding the seeds and stems. Cook the fresh corn in water in a saucepan for 5 minutes. Cool in ice water and cut off the kernels.

Combine the tomatillos, chiles and corn in a bowl. Add the garlic, basil, olive oil and vinegar. Season with salt and pepper. Chill for 2 hours or longer.

To prepare the cream, combine the bell peppers, garlic, shallot, wine and vinegar in a saucepan. Bring to a boil and reduce the heat. Simmer for 15 minutes. Stir in the cream and simmer for 10 minutes longer. Whisk in the butter gradually and season with salt and white pepper. Strain through a fine sieve and return to the saucepan to keep hot.

To prepare the fish, rub the mahi mahi with olive oil and season with salt and pepper. Grill for 4 minutes on each side.

Spoon the cream onto 6 serving plates. Place a portion of the fish on each plate and top with the salsa.

Serves six

PEPPER-CRUSTED SALMON

Soy Marinade

$^1/_4$ cup soy sauce
4 teaspoons fresh lemon juice
2 garlic cloves, minced
2 teaspoons brown sugar

Salmon

1 (2-pound) center-cut salmon fillet, skinned and cut into 4 portions
8 teaspoons coarsely ground pepper
$^1/_4$ cup olive oil

To prepare the marinade, combine the soy sauce, lemon juice, garlic and brown sugar in a sealable plastic bag and mix well.

To prepare the salmon, add the fillets to the marinade and marinate in the refrigerator for 30 minutes. Drain, discarding the marinade. Press the pepper onto both sides of the steaks.

Heat the olive oil in a heavy skillet over medium-high heat until hot but not smoking. Add the salmon and sauté for 2 minutes on each side or until the fish flakes easily. Remove to paper towels to drain.

Serves four

THE VARIETY OF FISH *in the market today is so vast that a trip to the fish counter can be daunting. There is a fish to suit everyone's taste. The flavor of fresh fish varies from the strong taste of salmon to the buttery delicate taste of halibut. The meatier varieties include tuna and swordfish. It is best not to buy fish that has been stored on ice; this will cause the flavor to deteriorate. The flesh of the fish should spring back when touched and should not smell fishy. Fish should always be cooked or frozen within 24 hours of purchase.*

GRILLED SALMON FILLETS WITH CUCUMBER AND DILL SAUCE

Cucumber and Dill Sauce

1   large cucumber, peeled, seeded and sliced
3   tablespoons chopped fresh dill
1   large scallion, thinly sliced
1 1/2 tablespoons balsamic vinegar
1/4 cup (2 ounces) sour cream or nonfat sour cream
1   teaspoon salt
1   teaspoon pepper

Salmon

1   to 2 teaspoons olive oil
2   (1/2 inch) salmon fillets

To prepare the sauce, combine the cucumber, dill, scallion, balsamic vinegar, sour cream, salt and pepper in a 1 1/2-quart saucepan and mix well. Bring to a boil and reduce the heat. Simmer for 2 to 3 minutes or until the flavors blend, stirring constantly.

To prepare the fish, brush the olive oil on both sides of each fillet. Grill over medium coals for 5 minutes on each side, turning frequently. Remove to a serving platter and spoon the sauce over the top.
Serves two

TEXAS WINE RECOMMENDATION: SPICEWOOD VINEYARDS SAUVIGNON BLANC

SNAPPER VERA CRUZ

2   pounds snapper fillets
1   teaspoon salt
1   teaspoon pepper
1   tablespoon olive oil
3   large tomatoes, chopped
1   green bell pepper, chopped
6   green onions, chopped
1/4 cup chopped pickled jalapeño peppers
1/4 cup green olives
4   garlic cloves, thinly sliced
     juice of 3 limes
2   tablespoons olive juice
1   tablespoon olive oil
1   lime, sliced

Rinse the snapper fillets under cold water and pat dry. Sprinkle with the salt and pepper. Coat a 9×13-inch baking dish with 1 tablespoon olive oil. Arrange the fillets in the dish and top with the tomatoes, bell pepper, green onions, jalapeño peppers, olives and garlic. Drizzle with the lime juice, olive juice and 1 tablespoon olive oil; top with the lime slices. Cover the fish with foil and bake at 375 degrees for 25 to 30 minutes or until the fish flakes easily.
Serves four to six

TEXAS WINE RECOMMENDATION: CROSS TIMBERS WINERY BLUSH

GRILLED SWORDFISH WITH GINGER LIME SAUCE

Ginger Lime Sauce

1	teaspoon chopped shallots
1	cup white wine
1	tablespoon grated gingerroot
1/3	cup heavy cream
1 1/2	cups (3 sticks) butter, chopped
	juice of 2 limes
1	tablespoon chopped cilantro
	salt and pepper to taste

Swordfish

4	slices peeled gingerroot
	olive oil
4	(8-ounce) swordfish steaks
	salt and pepper to taste

To prepare the sauce, combine the shallots, wine and grated gingerroot in a saucepan and bring to a boil. Cook until the liquid has evaporated. Stir in the cream and bring to a simmer. Whisk in the butter gradually. Remove the saucepan from the heat and add the lime juice and cilantro. Season with salt and pepper. Keep warm.

To prepare the fish, brush the gingerroot slices with olive oil and grill until golden brown. Season the swordfish steaks with salt and pepper. Grill over hot coals for 4 minutes on each side.

Remove the swordfish to serving plates and top each steak with a slice of grilled gingerroot. Spoon the sauce around the steaks. Serve hot.

You may substitute salmon for the swordfish in this recipe.

Serves four

CHIPOTLE TUNA TACOS

1	cup (8 ounces) sour cream
1/2	cup chopped red onion
1/2	cup chopped cilantro
2	chipotle peppers, minced
12	to 16 ounces ahi tuna steaks
	juice of 1 lime
2	tablespoons taco seasoning mix
2	tablespoons vegetable oil
8	corn or flour taco shells
	Mango Salsa (page 143)
	sliced avocado
	black olives

Mix the sour cream, onion, cilantro and chipotle peppers in a bowl. Cut the tuna into 3/4-inch pieces and combine with the lime juice and taco seasoning in a bowl. Heat the vegetable oil in a heavy skillet over medium-high heat. Add the tuna and sauté for 3 minutes for medium-rare or until done to taste.

Reduce the heat to low and stir in the sour cream mixture. Cook for 2 minutes or until heated through, stirring constantly; do not boil.

Heat the taco shells using the package directions. Spoon the tuna mixture into the shells and top with Mango Salsa, sliced avocado and black olives.
Serves four

A CHIPOTLE PEPPER *is a smoked jalapeño pepper. It is thought that the Aztecs smoked the peppers because the thick, fleshy jalapeño was prone to rot and was difficult to dry. The smoking allowed the peppers to be stored for long periods of time. Chipotles are considered to have a "medium" heat intensity compared to other peppers.*

BALSAMIC-GLAZED TUNA

Balsamic Glaze

1/4	cup fat-free chicken broth
1	tablespoon balsamic vinegar
4	teaspoons brown sugar
1	tablespoon soy sauce
1/2	teaspoon cornstarch

Tuna

4	(6-ounce) tuna steaks
1/4	teaspoon salt
1 1/4	teaspoons pepper
1/4	cup sliced green onions

To prepare the glaze, combine the chicken broth, balsamic vinegar, brown sugar, soy sauce and cornstarch in a small saucepan and mix until smooth. Bring to a boil and cook for 1 minute, stirring constantly. Keep warm.

To prepare the fish, sprinkle the tuna steaks with salt and pepper. Spray a grill pan with nonstick cooking spray and heat over medium-high heat. Place the tuna on the grill pan and cook for 3 minutes on each side for medium-rare or until done to taste. Remove from the heat. Place the tuna on serving plates and spoon the glaze over the top. Sprinkle with the green onions.

Serves four

TEXAS WINE RECOMMENDATION: MESSINA HOF WINERY JOHANNESBURG RIESLING

SPICY GRILLED SHRIMP

1	garlic clove, minced
1	teaspoon paprika
1	tablespoon coarse salt
1/2	teaspoon cayenne pepper
1 1/2	tablespoons olive oil
1	tablespoon fresh lemon juice
1 1/2	to 2 pounds shrimp, peeled
	lemon wedges

Mix the garlic, paprika, salt and cayenne pepper in a small bowl. Add the olive oil and lemon juice and mix to form a paste. Rinse the shrimp and pat dry. Spread the paste on the shrimp.

Place the grill rack close to coals or gas briquettes heated to high heat. Add the shrimp and grill for 2 to 3 minutes on each side. Serve immediately or at room temperature with lemon wedges.

You can also broil the shrimp if preferred.

Serves four to six

SHRIMP AND MUSHROOMS AU GRATIN

1	pound mushrooms, sliced
3	tablespoons butter
3	tablespoons flour
6	tablespoons dry sherry or marsala
2	cups light cream
1	teaspoon onion juice
1/4	teaspoon grated lemon zest
1	tablespoon chopped fresh parsley
	salt and pepper to taste
2	pounds peeled cooked shrimp, deveined
	freshly grated Parmesan cheese to taste
1/2	cup fine dry bread crumbs

Sauté the mushrooms in the butter in a saucepan until tender. Stir in the flour and cook until bubbly. Add the wine, cream, onion juice, lemon zest, parsley, salt and pepper. Cook over low heat until thickened and smooth, stirring constantly. Add the shrimp and cook until heated through. Spoon the mixture into 8 buttered ramekins. Top with Parmesan cheese and the bread crumbs. Bake at 400 degrees for 5 minutes or until the cheese is golden brown and the mixture is bubbly.

You may also bake in a baking dish for up to 15 minutes or until bubbly.

Serves eight

PENNE RUSTICA

1	small onion, chopped
1	red bell pepper, thinly sliced
	salt and pepper to taste
	olive oil
12	to 15 mushrooms, coarsely chopped or sliced
2	(15-ounce) cans chopped tomatoes with roasted garlic
2	(15-ounce) cans artichoke hearts, drained and quartered
1	pound uncooked penne
1 1/2	cups (6 ounces) grated Parmesan cheese
8	to 10 fresh basil leaves, julienned into 1/8-inch strips

Sauté the onion and bell pepper with salt and pepper in a small amount of olive oil in a heated skillet until the onion and bell pepper are tender. Add the mushrooms and sauté until tender. Add the undrained tomatoes, stirring to deglaze the skillet. Stir in the artichoke hearts and cook until heated through. Keep warm.

Cook the pasta in salted water using the package directions; drain. Add the tomato mixture and toss to mix well. Spoon immediately onto serving plates and top with the Parmesan cheese and basil.

You should not rinse the pasta after draining it for this recipe.

Serves eight to ten

TEXAS WINE RECOMMENDATION: CAP ROCK WINERY TOSCANA ROSSO RESERVE

SOUTHWESTERN LASAGNA

4	jalapeño peppers
2	cups chopped onions
1	cup chopped green bell pepper
1	cup chopped red bell pepper
5	garlic cloves, minced
2	cups chopped tomatoes
1 1/2	teaspoons ground cumin
1 1/2	teaspoons ground coriander
2	(16-ounce) cans black beans, rinsed and drained
1	cup (8 ounces) reduced-fat sour cream
1	egg
3	tablespoons chopped fresh cilantro
1	(16-ounce) jar chunky salsa
12	cooked lasagna noodles
2	cups (8 ounces) shredded Monterey Jack cheese

Cut the jalapeño peppers into halves lengthwise, discarding the seeds and membranes. Place skin side up on a foil-lined baking sheet and press to flatten. Broil for 4 minutes or until blackened. Place in a sealable plastic bag and seal. Let stand for 5 minutes. Remove the skins and chop the chiles. Reduce the oven temperature to 375 degrees.

Heat a large nonstick skillet over medium-high heat. Add the onions, bell peppers and garlic and sauté for 6 minutes. Stir in the tomatoes, cumin and coriander and sauté for 3 minutes. Add the chopped peppers and beans and cook for 3 minutes. Remove from the heat and cool for 10 minutes. Stir in the sour cream, egg and cilantro.

Spread 1/3 of the salsa in a 9×13-inch baking dish sprayed with nonstick cooking spray. Arrange 4 of the noodles in the prepared dish and layer with half the bean mixture, 1/2 cup of the cheese and 1/3 of the salsa. Repeat the layers and top with the remaining 4 noodles. Sprinkle with the remaining 1 cup cheese.

Bake, covered, at 375 degrees for 30 minutes. Remove the cover and bake for 15 minutes longer or until the cheese melts. Let stand for 5 minutes before serving.
Serves eight

HAVARTI PASTA

3	tablespoons olive oil
1¹/2	cups chopped onion
1	teaspoon minced garlic
3	(28-ounce) cans Italian plum tomatoes, drained
2	teaspoons dried basil
1¹/2	teaspoons crushed dried red pepper
2	cups canned reduced-sodium chicken broth
	salt and pepper to taste
1	pound uncooked penne or rigatoni
3	tablespoons olive oil
2¹/2	cups (10 ounces) shredded Havarti cheese
1/3	cup sliced black olives
1/3	cup (1¹/3 ounces) grated Parmesan cheese
1/4	cup finely chopped fresh basil

Heat 3 tablespoons olive oil in a large heavy saucepan over medium-high heat. Add the onion and garlic and sauté for 5 minutes or until the onion is translucent. Add the tomatoes, dried basil and crushed red pepper. Bring to a boil, stirring to break up the tomatoes with the back of the spoon. Stir in the chicken broth and return to a boil. Reduce the heat to medium and simmer for 1 hour and 10 minutes or until the mixture is reduced to 6 cups, stirring occasionally. Season with salt and pepper.

Cook the pasta al dente using the package directions. Drain and toss with 3 tablespoons olive oil in the same saucepan. Add the tomato mixture and toss to mix well. Stir in the Havarti cheese. Spoon into a 9×13-inch baking dish and sprinkle with the black olives and Parmesan cheese. Bake at 375 degrees for 30 minutes. Sprinkle with the fresh basil to serve.
Serves eight to ten

CREAMED SPINACH

Chef Steve DeShazo, founder of GourmetOnTheGo.com, has served more than ten million meals in his career. GourmetOnTheGo.com continues to be a leader in the industry as one of the largest personal chef services in the nation.

1/4	cup chopped onion
2	tablespoons butter, melted
2	garlic cloves, minced
3	tablespoons flour
1 1/4	cups milk
1 1/2	pounds spinach, blanched and drained
	salt and pepper to taste
	shredded Cheddar cheese

Sauté the onion in the butter in a skillet over medium heat until translucent. Add the garlic and sauté for 20 to 30 seconds or until the flavor is released. Whisk in the flour and cook until golden brown, whisking constantly.

Stir in the milk and cook until smooth and thickened, whisking constantly. Stir in the spinach and season with salt and pepper. Spoon into a baking dish and top with Cheddar cheese. Bake at 350 degrees until the cheese melts.

Serves four

GRILLED PORTOBELLO MUSHROOMS

Texas is known for its remarkable steak houses. One of the most famous is Chamberlain's Steak and Chop House. Chef Chamberlain has been preparing prime cuts in Dallas since 1993. No steak dinner would be complete without the perfect accompaniment, such as Grilled Portobello Mushrooms.

4   large portobello mushrooms
2   tablespoons olive oil
1   teaspoon chopped fresh rosemary
1   tablespoon minced garlic
        salt and pepper to taste
        balsamic vinegar

Rub the mushrooms with the olive oil and sprinkle with rosemary, garlic, salt and pepper. Place in a roasting pan. Roast at 375 degrees for 20 minutes. Remove from the oven and keep warm.

Heat a grill to medium-hot and brush the rack with a small amount of olive oil. Place the mushrooms on the rack and grill for 6 minutes or until tender, rotating every 2 minutes. Sprinkle with balsamic vinegar to serve.

Serves 4

CHEFS' RECIPES

ASPARAGUS AU GRATIN

1	pound fresh mushrooms
2	tablespoons butter
2	pounds fresh asparagus, cooked and cut into 1/2-inch pieces
5	eggs, hard-cooked and sliced
2	tablespoons butter
3	tablespoons flour
1 1/2	cups light cream
1	cup (4 ounces) shredded Cheddar cheese
1	teaspoon Worcestershire sauce
1	teaspoon salt
1/4	teaspoon pepper
	bread crumbs
	paprika to taste

Sauté the mushrooms in 2 tablespoons butter in a skillet until tender; drain. Add the asparagus and eggs and mix gently. Spoon into a greased baking dish. Melt 2 tablespoons butter in a saucepan. Stir in the flour and cook until bubbly. Add the cream and cook until thickened, stirring constantly. Stir in the Cheddar cheese, Worcestershire sauce, salt and pepper and cook until the cheese melts, stirring constantly. Pour over the asparagus mixture in the baking dish. Sprinkle bread crumbs around the edge of the dish and sprinkle the center generously with paprika. Bake at 350 degrees for 20 minutes or until bubbly.
Serves six to eight

TOMATO-TOPPED ASPARAGUS

2	tablespoons olive oil
2	tablespoons cider vinegar
2	tablespoons chopped fresh basil
1/2	teaspoon each salt and pepper
1	pound fresh asparagus
1/3	cup finely chopped tomato
	chopped fresh basil
	crumbled feta cheese or shaved Parmesan cheese

Combine the olive oil, vinegar, 2 tablespoons basil, salt and pepper in a small jar. Cover and shake to mix well. Snap off the tough ends of the asparagus. Place the spears in a vegetable steamer over boiling water. Steam, covered, for 4 to 6 minutes or just until tender.

Arrange the spears on a serving platter and sprinkle with the chopped tomato. Drizzle with the oil and vinegar mixture. Garnish with additional fresh basil, crumbled feta cheese or shaved Parmesan cheese.
Serves four

WALNUT AND MUSHROOM ASPARAGUS

1/2   cup walnuts
4   small green onions, chopped
2   cups sliced fresh mushrooms
6   tablespoons (3/4 stick) butter
      salt to taste
3   pounds fresh asparagus, cooked

Spread the walnuts in a shallow baking pan. Toast at 300 degrees for 10 minutes. Cool and grind coarsely. Sauté the green onions and mushrooms in the butter in a skillet until tender. Add the toasted walnuts and season with salt.

Drain the asparagus well and arrange on a serving platter. Spoon the mushroom mixture over the asparagus.
Serves eight

GREEN BEAN BUNDLES

1   pound fresh green beans, blanched
4   slices bacon
1/2   cup packed brown sugar
1/2   garlic clove, crushed
1/4   cup (1/2 stick) butter, melted

Arrange the beans into 8 bundles. Cut the bacon slices into halves and wrap 1/2 slice around each bean bundle; secure with wooden picks. Place in a baking pan.

Combine the brown sugar, garlic and butter in a small bowl and mix well. Spoon over the bean bundles. Bake at 350 degrees for 35 minutes.
Serves eight

RED PEPPER SAUCE *really perks up steamed asparagus. Chop 1 red bell pepper and 1 red onion and sauté in 2 tablespoons butter in a saucepan. Add 1 can chicken broth and simmer for 5 minutes. Process in a blender until smooth. Return to the saucepan and add a mixture of cornstarch and water. Cook until thickened, stirring constantly. Spoon onto a serving platter and arrange steamed asparagus in the sauce.*

GREEN BEANS WITH BALSAMIC VINAIGRETTE

1	pound fresh tender green beans
	salt to taste
1¹/2	tablespoons minced shallots
2	tablespoons Dijon mustard
1¹/2	tablespoons balsamic vinegar
¹/4	cup olive oil
¹/2	teaspoon lemon juice
	pepper to taste
2	tablespoons chopped fresh dill

Trim the ends of the beans. Cook in salted water in a saucepan for 8 to 10 minutes or until tender-crisp; drain and keep warm.

Combine the shallots, Dijon mustard, balsamic vinegar, olive oil and lemon juice in a small saucepan. Cook over low heat until heated through, stirring to mix well. Season with salt and pepper. Add to the beans and toss to coat well. Sprinkle with the dill and serve immediately.
Serves four to six

GREEN BEANS WITH FETA AND PECANS

¹/3	cup white vinegar
¹/2	teaspoon minced garlic
1	teaspoon dillweed
¹/4	teaspoon salt
¹/4	teaspoon freshly ground pepper
2/3	cup olive oil
2	pounds green beans
¹/2	cup chopped red onion
1	cup (4 ounces) crumbled feta cheese
1	cup pecans, toasted and coarsely chopped

Combine the vinegar, garlic, dillweed, salt and pepper in a bowl and mix well. Drizzle in the olive oil, whisking constantly to blend well.

Trim the green beans and cut into 1-inch pieces. Cook in water in a saucepan just until tender-crisp; drain. Immerse in cold water, drain and pat dry. Place in a shallow serving bowl and sprinkle with the onion, feta cheese and pecans. Add the vinegar and oil mixture at serving time and toss gently to coat well.
Serves four to six

The photograph for this recipe is on page 163.

BARRACHO BEANS

1	pound dried pinto beans
1	(12-ounce) can beer
1	medium onion, chopped
5	slices bacon
1	(15-ounce) can diced tomatoes with green chiles
1	tablespoon chopped garlic
2	teaspoons ground cumin
1	tablespoon salt
1	teaspoon pepper
2	cups chopped cilantro
	shredded cheese and chopped green onions

Combine the beans with enough water to cover by 1 to 2 inches in a bowl and soak for 8 to 10 hours; drain. Combine with the beer in a large saucepan and add enough water to cover by 1 to 2 inches. Add the onion and bacon. Bring to a boil and reduce the heat to medium. Simmer for 1 hour or until the beans are tender.

Reduce the heat to low and add the tomatoes with green chiles, garlic, cumin, salt and pepper. Simmer until serving time on the stove top or in a slow cooker set on Low. Add the cilantro just before serving. Serve in bowls and garnish with cheese and green onions.
Serves fifteen to twenty

BROCCOLI AND ARTICHOKE CASSEROLE

1	(14-ounce) can artichoke hearts, drained and quartered
1/2	cup (1 stick) butter, melted
8	ounces cream cheese, softened
1 1/2	teaspoons lemon juice
2	(10-ounce) packages frozen chopped broccoli, cooked and drained
1	cup saltine cracker crumbs

Place the artichoke hearts in a greased 1 1/2-quart baking dish. Combine the butter, cream cheese and lemon juice in a bowl and mix until smooth. Add the broccoli and mix gently. Spoon over the artichokes and top with the cracker crumbs. Bake at 350 degrees for 25 minutes.
Serves six

THE HERITAGE FARMSTEAD, *which opened in 1986, offers visitors a history lesson in living color. The 1891 Victorian residence features a four-acre complex with crops, gardens, a windmill, and a dozen original outbuildings. More than 15,000 visitors tour the museum each year, getting a first-hand look at the turn-of-the-century farming that helped shape Plano into the community it is today. The museum has received a State of Texas Historical Marker and a listing in the National Register of Historic Places.*

BROCCOLI TIMBALES

1	pound fresh broccoli
3	eggs
1	cup heavy cream
1	tablespoon lemon juice
1/4	teaspoon salt
	pepper to taste
	chopped tomato and green onions

Trim the broccoli stalks and chop the florets. Peel the stalks with a vegetable peeler and cut into 1-inch pieces; cut the pieces into halves lengthwise. Bring 1/2 inch of water to a boil in a medium saucepan over high heat. Reduce the heat to medium-low and add the chopped broccoli stems. Simmer, covered, for 10 minutes or until tender-crisp.

Remove the stems to a blender or food processor with a slotted spoon. Add the eggs and process until smooth. Add the cream and pulse until blended. Add the lemon juice, salt and pepper and pulse once.

Add the florets to the saucepan and simmer, covered, for 5 minutes or until tender-crisp and bright green. Remove to a cutting board and reserve 6 small flowerets for garnish. Chop the remaining florets and add to the food processor; pulse several times to mix.

Spoon the mixture into 6 buttered 6-ounce ramekins and arrange in a 9×13-inch baking pan. Add enough boiling water to the baking pan to reach halfway up the sides of the ramekins. Bake at 375 degrees for 25 to 30 minutes or until a knife inserted into the centers comes out clean. Top with the reserved broccoli florets and garnish with chopped tomato and green onions. Let stand for 5 minutes and serve in the ramekins.
Serves six

SASSY BRUSSELS SPROUTS

1	pound Brussels sprouts
	salt to taste
1/2	cup chopped onion
2	tablespoons butter
1	tablespoon flour
1	tablespoon brown sugar
1/2	teaspoon dry mustard
1	teaspoon salt
1/2	cup milk
1	cup (8 ounces) sour cream

Cook the Brussels sprouts in a small amount of salted water in a covered saucepan for 10 to 15 minutes or until tender-crisp; drain well.

Sauté the onion in the butter in a medium saucepan until tender but not brown. Stir in the flour, brown sugar, dry mustard and 1 teaspoon salt and cook until bubbly. Add the milk and cook until thickened, stirring constantly. Stir in the sour cream. Add the Brussels sprouts and mix gently. Cook just until heated through; do not boil.
Serves six

CARROTS AND CAPERS

1   pound carrots
2   tablespoons olive oil
1   garlic clove, crushed
2   tablespoons chopped parsley
1/2 cup water
2   tablespoons drained capers
1/4 teaspoon salt
     pepper to taste

Cut the carrots into 3-inch sticks. Heat the olive oil in a large skillet. Add the garlic and sauté until golden brown. Add the carrots and parsley and mix to coat well. Add the water and cook, partially covered, until the carrots are tender and the water evaporates. Cook until the carrots are light brown. Add the capers, salt and pepper and toss to mix well.
Serves eight to ten

The photograph for this recipe is on page 121.

CARROT SOUFFLÉ

Carrots

2   pounds carrots, peeled and chopped
6   eggs
6   tablespoons flour
1   cup sugar
1/2 cup (1 stick) butter, melted
2   teaspoons baking powder
2   teaspoons vanilla extract
1/2 teaspoon nutmeg
1/2 teaspoon cinnamon

Crunchy Topping

1/2 cup crushed cornflakes
6   tablespoons brown sugar
1/4 cup (1/2 stick) butter, softened
1/4 cup chopped nuts
1/2 teaspoon nutmeg
1/2 teaspoon cinnamon

To prepare the carrots, boil or steam them until very tender; drain. Combine with the eggs in a blender or food processor and process until smooth. Add the flour, sugar, butter, baking powder, vanilla, nutmeg and cinnamon and process until well mixed. Spoon into a greased 9×13-inch baking dish.

To prepare the topping, mix the cornflakes, brown sugar, butter, nuts, nutmeg and cinnamon in a bowl. Sprinkle over the carrot mixture. Bake at 350 degrees for 45 minutes.

You may reduce the recipe by half to serve four.
Serves eight to ten

GRATINÉE OF CAULIFLOWER

	florets of 1 large head cauliflower
4	garlic cloves, minced
6	tablespoons ($3/4$ stick) unsalted butter
4	ounces thinly sliced prosciutto, julienned
2	tablespoons unbleached flour
$1^1/2$	cups heavy cream
	salt, cayenne pepper and black pepper to taste
$1^1/2$	cups (6 ounces) shredded Swiss cheese
$1/2$	cup chopped fresh parsley

Cut the cauliflower florets lengthwise into $1/4$-inch slices. Sauté the garlic in the butter in a large skillet over medium heat for 2 minutes. Add the prosciutto and sauté for 2 minutes. Add the cauliflower and sauté for 3 to 4 minutes or just until tender-crisp. Stir in the flour and cook until bubbly, stirring constantly. Add the cream, salt, cayenne pepper and black pepper. Bring to a boil, stirring constantly; remove from the heat.

Spoon into a shallow baking dish. Top with the Swiss cheese and parsley. Bake at 350 degrees for 3 minutes or until the cauliflower mixture is bubbly and the top is light brown.

Serves six to eight

BAKED EGGPLANT

2	medium eggplant
	salt to taste
$1/2$	medium white onion, chopped
2	eggs, lightly beaten
1	cup (4 ounces) grated Parmesan cheese or shredded sharp Cheddar cheese
	pepper to taste
2	cups fine bread crumbs
3	to 4 tablespoons melted butter

Peel and chop the eggplant. Cook in a small amount of salted water in a saucepan until tender; drain. Add the onion, eggs, Parmesan cheese and pepper and mix gently.

Toss the bread crumbs with the melted butter in a bowl. Add half the bread crumbs to the eggplant mixture and mix gently.

Spoon the eggplant mixture into a greased 2-quart baking dish. Top with the remaining buttered bread crumbs. Bake at 350 degrees for 30 to 45 minutes or until bubbly.

Serves eight to ten

TWICE-BAKED POTATOES WITH MUSHROOMS AND CHEESE

6	russet potatoes
12	ounces fresh mushrooms, chopped
1	tablespoon butter
2	large green onions, chopped
4	ounces cream cheese, softened
1/2	cup (4 ounces) sour cream
1/4	cup (1/2 stick) butter, softened
1/2	cup (2 ounces) shredded white Cheddar cheese
	salt and pepper to taste
3/4	cup (3 ounces) shredded white Cheddar cheese

Pierce the potatoes with a knife and place on the oven rack. Bake at 375 degrees for 1 hour or until tender.

Sauté the mushrooms in 1 tablespoon butter in a heavy skillet over medium heat for 6 to 8 minutes or until light brown. Add the green onions and sauté for 1 minute longer.

Cut the potatoes into halves lengthwise. Scoop the pulp into a bowl, reserving the shells. Add the cream cheese, sour cream and 1/4 cup butter and mix until smooth. Add the mushroom mixture and 1/2 cup Cheddar cheese. Season with salt and pepper.

Spoon the potato mixture into the reserved potato shells and sprinkle with 3/4 cup Cheddar cheese. Place in a baking pan and bake at 375 degrees for 25 minutes or until the cheese melts.

Serves twelve

TOP BAKED POTATOES *with Savory Cheese Sauce for a quick dinner solution. Melt 1/4 cup butter in a saucepan and blend in 1/4 cup flour. Cook until bubbly, stirring constantly. Add 2 cups milk and cook until thickened and smooth, stirring constantly. Add 1 1/2 cups shredded sharp Cheddar cheese and cook until melted and smooth. Season with a few drops of Tabasco sauce, 1/2 teaspoon Worcestershire sauce, 1 teaspoon salt, and cayenne pepper to taste. Add 1/2 cup chopped green onions and serve over baked potatoes.*

HEART'S DELIGHT POTATOES

4   medium potatoes
1¹/2   cups light cream
¹/2   cup (1 stick) butter
2   cups (8 ounces) shredded medium or sharp Cheddar cheese
       salt and pepper to taste
1   cup (8 ounces) sour cream
¹/2   cup chopped green onions
6   to 8 slices bacon, crisp-fried and crumbled
       paprika to taste

Cook the potatoes in water to cover in a large saucepan until tender; drain and cool. Peel the potatoes and grate into a bowl. Combine the cream, butter and cheese in a double boiler and cook until the butter and cheese melt, stirring to blend well. Add to the potatoes and season with salt and pepper; mix well.

Spoon into a 9×13-inch baking dish and bake at 350 degrees for 30 minutes. Top with the sour cream, green onions and bacon. Sprinkle with paprika if desired. Bake for 5 minutes longer.

Serves eight

SQUASH DRESSING

1   package Mexican corn bread mix
1   pound sausage
1   medium white onion, finely chopped
1¹/2   cups chopped squash
1   (10-ounce) can cream of mushroom soup
2   cups milk
¹/4   cup chopped green onions (optional)
1   teaspoon ground sage
       salt and pepper to taste
1   cup (4 ounces) shredded Cheddar cheese

Prepare the corn bread mix using the package directions. Brown the sausage in a skillet, stirring until crumbly; drain. Add the onion and cook until the onion is tender. Cook the squash in water to cover in a saucepan until tender; drain.

Crumble the corn bread into a bowl. Add the sausage mixture, squash, soup, milk, green onions, sage, salt and pepper and mix well. Stir in half the cheese.

Spoon the mixture into a 9×13-inch baking dish and bake at 350 degrees for 20 minutes. Sprinkle with the remaining cheese and bake for 5 minutes longer or until the cheese melts.

Serves eight

SAN ANTONIO SQUASH CASSEROLE

6   squash, peeled and sliced
1   onion, chopped
1   tablespoon butter
     salt and pepper to taste
2   cups (16 ounces) sour cream
1   (10-ounce) can cream of mushroom soup
1   cup chopped green chiles
1   (15-ounce) package corn chips, crushed
2   cups (8 ounces) shredded Cheddar cheese

Cook the squash with the onion in water to just cover in a saucepan until tender. Mash the squash and add the butter, salt and pepper. Cook over medium heat until the mixture is nearly dry. Mix the sour cream, soup and green chiles in a bowl. Add to the squash and mix well.

Sprinkle 1/3 of the corn chips into a greased 2-quart baking dish. Spread half the squash mixture in the prepared dish. Repeat the layers and top with the shredded Cheddar cheese and remaining chips. Bake at 350 degrees for 30 minutes or until the cheese is melted.
Serves eight to ten

SWEET POTATO SOUFFLÉ

6   medium sweet potatoes, about 31/2 pounds
       salt to taste
1/2   cup (1 stick) butter, softened
1   cup each sugar and heavy cream
6   eggs
1/2   teaspoon each vanilla extract and cinnamon
1   teaspoon salt
11/2   cups miniature marshmallows (optional)

Cook the sweet potatoes in salted water in a saucepan until very tender; drain. Cool and peel the sweet potatoes. Spoon into a mixing bowl and add the butter, sugar, cream, eggs, vanilla, cinnamon and 1 teaspoon salt. Beat at low speed until smooth.

Spoon into a greased 3-quart soufflé dish or baking dish. Bake at 375 degrees for 20 minutes. Reduce the oven temperature to 350 degrees and bake for 40 minutes longer. Sprinkle with the marshmallows. Broil for 1 minute or until the marshmallows are golden brown.
Serves ten to twelve

SWEET POTATOES *are firmly rooted in Texas. They were first cultivated in Texas by the Spanish and became the state's leading vegetable crop throughout the 1920s and 1930s. Sweet potatoes are hailed for being a tasty source of beta-carotene, vitamin A, and vitamin C. Experts say that the "perfect" sweet potato is 21/2 inches in diameter, 6 to 8 inches long, and has a smooth skin and good color.*

CHEESY CHILE ZUCCHINI BAKE

2	pounds zucchini, sliced
1	medium onion, chopped
3/4	cup (3 ounces) shredded Swiss cheese
3/4	cup (3 ounces) shredded Cheddar cheese
1	(4-ounce) can chopped green chiles
1	cup (8 ounces) sour cream
	salt and pepper to taste
1/2	cup bread crumbs
1/4	cup (1 ounce) grated Parmesan cheese
2	teaspoons butter

Cook the zucchini with the onion in water to cover in a large saucepan until tender; drain. Remove to a buttered baking dish.

Combine the Swiss cheese, Cheddar cheese, green chiles, sour cream, salt and pepper in a small bowl and mix well. Spread over the zucchini mixture. Mix the bread crumbs and Parmesan cheese in a small bowl and sprinkle over the top. Dot with the butter. Bake at 350 degrees for 25 minutes.

Serves eight

SESAME ZUCCHINI

1/4	cup chopped onion
1/2	garlic clove, minced
1/4	cup (1/2 stick) butter
6	zucchini, sliced diagonally
1/2	cup cherry tomatoes, cut into halves
	salt and pepper to taste
2	tablespoons toasted sesame seeds
1/4	cup chopped parsley

Sauté the onion and garlic in the butter in a saucepan. Add the zucchini and sauté for 5 minutes. Add the tomatoes. Cook, covered, for 5 minutes. Season with salt and pepper. Add the sesame seeds and parsley at serving time and mix gently.

Serves six to eight

EVER WONDER *how the Texas 1015 onion got its name? In this case, timing is everything. The 1015 onion from South Texas is seeded each year on October 15, or 10/15. This rather large onion is available only from mid-April through May. It is known primarily for its sweet and mild taste, but also for its attractive appearance due to its single center.*

SPINACH SOUFFLÉ

2	(10-ounce) packages frozen chopped spinach
1 1/3	cups cottage cheese
2	cups (8 ounces) shredded Cheddar cheese
1/4	cup (1/2 stick) butter
3	eggs, beaten
	salt and pepper to taste

Cook the spinach using the package directions; drain well. Combine with the cottage cheese, Cheddar cheese, butter, eggs, salt and pepper in a bowl and mix well. Spoon into a greased 5×9-inch baking dish. Bake at 350 degrees for 1 hour. Let stand for 5 to 10 minutes before serving.
Serves six

SPINACH AND FETA RICE

1	cup uncooked rice
1	cup chicken broth
1	cup water
1	medium onion, chopped
1	cup sliced mushrooms
2	garlic cloves, minced
1	tablespoon lemon juice
1/2	teaspoon oregano
6	cups chopped spinach
1	cup (4 ounces) crumbled feta cheese
1/2	teaspoon pepper
1/4	cup chopped pimento (optional)

Combine the rice, chicken broth and water in a saucepan and bring to a boil. Stir the mixture and reduce the heat. Simmer, covered, for 15 to 20 minutes or until the rice is tender and the liquid is absorbed.

Sauté the onion, mushrooms and garlic in a large nonstick skillet sprayed with nonstick cooking spray until the onion is tender. Stir in the lemon juice and oregano.

Combine the rice, spinach, feta cheese and pepper in a bowl. Add the mushroom mixture and toss lightly until the spinach is wilted. Garnish with the pimento.
Serves six

WILD RICE PARTY DISH

1   cup uncooked long grain and wild rice mix
1/2   cup (1 stick) butter
2   tablespoons chopped onion
1/2   cup slivered almonds
8   ounces mushrooms, sliced
3   tablespoons sherry
1   teaspoon salt
3   cups chicken broth or beef broth

Combine the rice, butter, onion, almonds, mushrooms, sherry and salt in a heavy saucepan. Cook for 20 minutes, stirring frequently. Spoon into a 2-quart baking dish. Add the chicken broth. Bake at 325 degrees for 1 hour.

To prepare for a party, you may prepare the dish and chill it, covered, until ready to bake. Let stand at room temperature for 15 minutes and bake as suggested.

Serves six

HOMINY CASSEROLE

1   onion, finely chopped
1   garlic clove, minced
1   tablespoon corn oil
1   (16-ounce) can white hominy, drained
1   (16-ounce) can yellow hominy, drained
1/2   cup (2 ounces) shredded Cheddar cheese
1   (4-ounce) can chopped green chiles
3/4   cup (6 ounces) sour cream
1/2   teaspoon cumin
1/2   teaspoon salt

Sauté the onion and garlic in the corn oil in a skillet until tender. Remove from the heat and add the hominy, Cheddar cheese, green chiles, sour cream, cumin and salt and mix well. Spoon into an oiled 2-quart baking dish. Bake at 350 degrees for 15 to 20 minutes or until heated through.

You may prepare the dish in advance and store in the refrigerator until baking time. Allow for a longer baking time.

Serves six

SOUTHERN CORN BREAD DRESSING

2	Red Delicious apples, peeled and chopped
3	cups chopped celery
2	cups chopped onions
1¹/₂	cups (3 sticks) butter
4	cups crumbled corn bread
3	cups torn fresh white bread
2	tablespoons poultry seasoning
1¹/₂	tablespoons dried sage
1¹/₂	teaspoons salt, or to taste
1	tablespoon pepper
2	eggs, beaten
8	cups (about) chicken broth

Sauté the apples, celery and onions in the butter in a skillet until very tender but not brown. Combine the crumbled corn bread and white bread in a large bowl. Add the apple mixture, poultry seasoning, sage, salt and pepper and mix well. Adjust the seasonings. Add the eggs and mix well. Stir in enough chicken broth to make a fairly thin mixture.

Spoon the dressing into a large baking pan. Bake at 350 degrees for 1 hour. Serve immediately.

This dish is best made with broth using the drippings from roasting a turkey.

Serves eight to ten

HOMINY, CORN, *and cornmeal were hot commodities back in Plano's early years. They were considered the second most important part of the diet, next to wild game. Corn had several valuable uses. In fact, every part of the vegetable was put to use. The shucks were used to make mops, rugs, mattresses, hats, and even children's toys.*

FESTIVE HOLIDAY STUFFING

1/2	cup chopped onion
1/2	cup chopped celery
2	tablespoons butter
8	cups cubed day-old egg bread
1	cup fresh orange juice
3	seedless oranges, peeled and chopped
2	tablespoons grated orange zest
3	apples, coarsely chopped
1	cup fresh cranberries
1	cup chopped fresh parsley
1	tablespoon minced fresh thyme
1	tablespoon minced fresh sage
	salt and pepper to taste
	chicken broth or vegetable broth

Sauté the onion and celery in the butter in a large heavy skillet over high heat until tender. Combine with the bread cubes in a large bowl. Add the orange juice, oranges, orange zest, apples, cranberries, parsley, thyme and sage and toss to mix well. Season with salt and pepper.

Add enough chicken broth to moisten the mixture without making it soggy. Spoon into a large greased baking dish. Bake at 350 degrees for 45 to 60 minutes or until heated through and golden brown.

Serves eight to ten

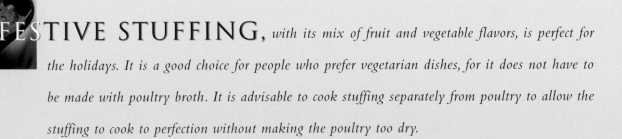

FESTIVE STUFFING, *with its mix of fruit and vegetable flavors, is perfect for the holidays. It is a good choice for people who prefer vegetarian dishes, for it does not have to be made with poultry broth. It is advisable to cook stuffing separately from poultry to allow the stuffing to cook to perfection without making the poultry too dry.*

YANKEE OYSTER DRESSING

1	pint oysters in liquid
1	medium onion, finely chopped
2	ribs celery, finely chopped
	butter
1	(16-ounce) package seasoned bread dressing mix, not cubed dressing mix
4	cups chicken broth or turkey broth

Simmer the oysters in their own liquid in a saucepan over medium-low heat just until the edges curl. Chop the oysters coarsely. Sauté the onion and celery in butter in a saucepan until tender. Add the oysters and dressing mix and mix well. Add enough chicken broth to moisten the mixture without making it soggy.

Spoon the dressing into a 2-quart baking dish and cover with foil. Bake at 350 degrees for 30 to 40 minutes or just until heated through, removing the foil during the last 10 minutes to brown.

Serves eight

BAKED FRUIT COMPOTE

1	(16-ounce) can dark sweet cherries
1/2	cup packed brown sugar
1	tablespoon cornstarch
2 1/2	tablespoons lemon juice
1/4	cup orange juice
1	(29-ounce) can sliced peaches, drained
6	ounces dried apricots
6	ounces dried pitted plums, cut into halves

Drain the cherries, reserving the cherries and the juice. Mix the brown sugar and cornstarch in a bowl. Add the cherry juice, lemon juice and orange juice gradually, stirring to mix well.

Combine the cherries, peaches, apricots and plums in a 2-quart baking dish. Pour the cherry juice mixture over the fruit. Bake, covered, at 350 degrees for 45 minutes or until the apricots are tender. Serve warm with baked chicken or turkey, ham or pork.

Serves eight

LASTING IMPRESSIONS

CHOCOLATE MELTING CAKES

Neiman Marcus is an upscale Dallas-based retailer whose doors first opened in 1907. The store is world famous for its customer service and quality offerings. It also hosts visitors at the Zodiac Room and Mariposa's restaurants.

8	ounces bittersweet chocolate or semisweet chocolate, chopped
6	tablespoons (3/4 stick) unsalted butter
1/2	cup flour
1/2	cup plus 2 tablespoons sugar
1	teaspoon salt
4	eggs

Combine the chocolate and butter in a heavy saucepan. Cook over low heat until melted, stirring until smooth. Cool to room temperature.

Mix the flour, sugar and salt in a large bowl. Beat in the eggs 1 at a time. Beat for 5 minutes or until the mixture is pale yellow and forms slowly dissolving ribbons when the beaters are lifted. Fold in the chocolate mixture. Chill in the refrigerator for 8 hours or longer.

Butter individual soufflé dishes or molds and sprinkle with additional sugar. Spoon the chocolate batter into the dishes. Bake at 325 degrees for 15 minutes or until the cakes are set on the top but a tester inserted in the center comes out with thick, wet batter still attached. Cool on wire racks. Loosen from the dishes with a knife and remove to serving plates.
Serves eight

TEXAS WINE RECOMMENDATION: LA BUENA VIDA WALNUT CREEK CELLARS 1998 VINTAGE PORT

PEPPERMINT PROFITEROLES

Maggiano's Little Italy serves old-world and new-world southern Italian cuisine. This family-style restaurant has a warm and inviting atmosphere. In business since 1991, Maggiano's has two locations in the Dallas area.

6	tablespoons (3/4 stick) butter
3/4	cup water
	pinch of salt
1 1/4	cups flour
4	eggs
10	scoops peppermint ice cream
1/2	cup hot fudge sauce
2	peppermint candy canes, broken

Combine the butter, water and salt in a saucepan and bring to a boil. Reduce the heat and add the flour all at once. Stir with a wooden spoon for 3 to 5 minutes or until the mixture forms a ball and pulls away from the side of the saucepan; a thin layer will adhere to the bottom of the saucepan.

Remove to a mixing bowl. Beat in the eggs 1 at a time with a paddle attachment. Scoop the mixture onto a baking parchment-lined baking sheet with an ice cream scoop. Bake at 425 degrees for 15 minutes or until puffed and light brown. Reduce the oven temperature to 325 degrees and bake for 15 to 20 minutes longer or until dry inside. Remove to a wire rack to cool.

Slice off the top 1/4 of each profiterole and reserve for a cap. Scoop the ice cream into the profiteroles and replace the tops. Place on dessert plates and drizzle with the hot fudge sauce. Garnish with the peppermint candy.
Serves ten

CHEFS' RECIPES

APPLE CAKE WITH CARAMEL SAUCE

Cake

3	eggs
1/2	cup vegetable oil
1/2	cup applesauce
2	cups flour
2	cups sugar
1	teaspoon baking soda
1	teaspoon vanilla extract
2	teaspoons cinnamon
1/2	teaspoon salt
4	cups chopped apples

Caramel Sauce

1/2	cup (1 stick) butter
1/2	cup sugar
1/2	cup packed brown sugar
1	tablespoon flour
1/2	cup cream
1	teaspoon vanilla extract

To prepare the cake, combine the eggs, vegetable oil and applesauce in a mixing bowl and beat lightly. Add the flour, sugar, baking soda, vanilla, cinnamon and salt and mix well. Fold in the apples. Spoon into a greased 9×13-inch cake pan. Bake at 350 degrees for 45 to 60 minutes or until the cake tests done.

To prepare the sauce, melt the butter in a saucepan. Add the sugar, brown sugar, flour, cream and vanilla and mix well. Bring to a boil over medium heat and cook for 2 minutes. Serve warm over the cake.

You may prepare the caramel sauce in advance and reheat to serve.

Serves twelve to fifteen

CLASSIC CARROT CAKE

Cake

2	cups flour
2	teaspoons baking soda
2¹/2	teaspoons cinnamon
1	teaspoon salt
2	cups sugar
1¹/2	cups vegetable oil
4	eggs
3	cups grated carrots
2	teaspoons vanilla extract

Cream Cheese Frosting

¹/2	cup (1 stick) butter, softened
8	ounces cream cheese, softened
1	(1-pound) package confectioners' sugar
2	teaspoons vanilla extract
	milk

To prepare the cake, sift the flour, baking soda, cinnamon and salt together. Combine the sugar, vegetable oil and eggs in a bowl and beat until smooth. Add the flour mixture and mix well. Fold in the carrots and vanilla.

Spoon the batter into 3 greased and floured 8-inch cake pans. Bake at 325 degrees for 45 minutes. Cool in the pans for 5 minutes; then remove to wire racks to cool completely.

To prepare the frosting, combine the butter and cream cheese in a bowl and beat until light. Add the confectioners' sugar and vanilla and beat until fluffy. Add enough milk as needed for the desired consistency, beating until smooth. Spread between the layers and over the top and side of the cake.

Serves twelve

TEXAS WINE RECOMMENDATION: SISTER CREEK VINEYARDS MUSCAT CANELLI

FLOURLESS CHOCOLATE CAKE WITH
CHOCOLATE GLAZE AND RASPBERRY COULIS

Raspberry Coulis

2	cups fresh raspberries
1/4	cup kirsch
2	tablespoons lemon juice
1	cup confectioners' sugar

Cake

2	cups (12 ounces) semisweet chocolate chips
3/4	cup (1 1/2 sticks) unsalted butter, chopped
6	egg whites
6	tablespoons sugar
6	egg yolks
6	tablespoons sugar
2	teaspoons vanilla extract

Chocolate Glaze and Garnish

1/2	cup heavy cream
1/2	cup dark corn syrup
1 1/2	cups (9 ounces) semisweet chocolate chips
	fresh raspberries

To prepare the coulis, combine the raspberries, liqueur, lemon juice and confectioners' sugar in a blender or food processor. Process until smooth. Strain into a bowl to remove the seeds. Spoon into a bowl and store, covered, in the refrigerator.

To prepare the cake, line the bottom of a buttered 9-inch springform pan with baking parchment and butter the parchment. Wrap the outside of the pan with foil.

Combine the chocolate chips and butter in a heavy saucepan and cook over low heat until melted, stirring constantly to blend. Cool to lukewarm, stirring frequently.

Beat the egg whites in a bowl until soft peaks form. Add 6 tablespoons sugar gradually and beat until medium-firm peaks form. Beat the egg yolks with 6 tablespoons sugar in a large bowl for 3 minutes or until light yellow and thick. Fold in the chocolate mixture and vanilla. Fold in the egg whites 1/3 at a time.

Spoon the batter into the prepared springform pan. Bake at 350 degrees for 50 minutes or until a tester comes out nearly clean. Cool in the pan on a wire rack; the cake will fall as it cools. Press down the top of the cake to even the surface. Loosen from the pan with a small knife and invert onto a cake round; remove the baking parchment.

To prepare the glaze, combine the cream and corn syrup in a medium saucepan and bring to a simmer. Remove from the heat and whisk in the chocolate chips until melted and smooth. Place the cake on a wire rack over a baking sheet. Spread 1/2 cup of the glaze smoothly over the top and side of the cake. Freeze for 3 minutes or until the glaze is almost set. Pour the remaining glaze over the cake and smooth. Place on a platter and chill for 1 hour or until the glaze is firm.

To serve, let the cake stand until room temperature and cut into wedges. Place on serving plates swirled with the coulis. Garnish with fresh raspberries.
Serves ten to twelve

BLACK RUSSIAN CAKE

Cake

1	(2-layer) package deep chocolate cake mix
1	(4 1/2-ounce) package chocolate or chocolate fudge instant pudding mix
1/2	cup vegetable oil
4	eggs
3/4	cup strong brewed coffee
6	tablespoons Kahlúa
6	tablespoons Crème de Cacao

Mocha Glaze

1	tablespoon strong brewed coffee
1	cup confectioners' sugar
1	tablespoon Kahlúa
1	tablespoon Crème de Cacao

To prepare the cake, combine the cake mix, pudding mix, vegetable oil, eggs, coffee and liqueurs in a mixing bowl. Beat at medium speed for 4 minutes. Spoon into a greased and floured 10-inch tube pan. Bake at 350 degrees for 45 to 50 minutes or until a wooden pick inserted into the center tests done. Cool in the pan for 5 minutes; then invert onto a wire rack.

To prepare the glaze, combine the coffee, confectioners' sugar and liqueurs in a bowl and mix well. Poke holes in the cake and spoon the glaze over the top, allowing the glaze to soak in.

Serves sixteen

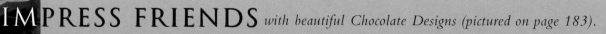

IMPRESS FRIENDS *with beautiful Chocolate Designs (pictured on page 183).*

Melt 4 ounces of semisweet chocolate chips in a double boiler or microwave and remove from the heat. Spoon into a paper cone or plastic bottle with a fine tip and squeeze the chocolate into thin lines on waxed paper to create the designs of your choice. You can draw the designs freehand or place a design under the waxed paper and trace it with the chocolate. Place the chocolate designs in the refrigerator or freezer to set. Remove the waxed paper gently from the back, handling the chocolate as little as possible. Use the designs to garnish desserts for a special touch.

CHOCOLATE ROULADE

Cake

1/2	cup baking cocoa
1/4	cup cake flour
3/4	teaspoon baking powder
4	eggs, at room temperature
3/4	cup sugar
1	teaspoon vanilla extract
1/2	teaspoon salt
	confectioners' sugar

Whipped Cream Filling

1 1/2	cups whipping cream
1/2	cup confectioners' sugar
1	teaspoon vanilla extract
	confectioners' sugar

To prepare the cake, line a greased 10×15-inch jelly roll pan with baking parchment and butter the parchment. Mix the baking cocoa, flour and baking powder together. Beat the eggs in a bowl until smooth. Add the sugar and beat until pale yellow and thick. Beat in the vanilla and salt. Fold in the flour mixture.

Spoon the batter into the prepared jelly roll pan. Bake at 400 degrees for 8 minutes. Cool in the pan for 2 minutes and invert onto a cloth dusted with confectioners' sugar; remove the baking parchment. Roll the cake in the towel from the narrow side and let stand until cool.

To prepare the filling, whip the cream in a mixing bowl until soft peaks form. Add 1/2 cup confectioners' sugar and vanilla and beat until smooth. Unroll the cake and spread with the whipped cream mixture and reroll the cake to enclose the filling. Place on a serving plate and sprinkle with additional confectioners' sugar.

Serves ten

CHOCOLATE SHEET CAKE

Cake

2	cups flour
2	cups sugar
1	cup (2 sticks) margarine
3	tablespoons baking cocoa
1	cup water
2	eggs, beaten
1/2	cup buttermilk
1	teaspoon baking soda
1	teaspoon vanilla extract
1/4	teaspoon salt

Chocolate Buttermilk Frosting

1/2	cup (1 stick) margarine
1/4	cup baking cocoa
6	tablespoons buttermilk
1	(1-pound) package confectioners' sugar
1	teaspoon vanilla extract

To prepare the cake, mix the flour and sugar in a large bowl. Combine the margarine, baking cocoa and water in a saucepan and bring to a boil, stirring to mix well. Add to the flour mixture and mix well. Beat in the eggs, buttermilk, baking soda, vanilla and salt. Spoon into a 10×15-inch baking sheet with sides. Bake at 350 degrees for 20 to 30 minutes or until the cake tests done.

To prepare the frosting, combine the margarine, baking cocoa and buttermilk in a saucepan. Bring to a boil, stirring to mix well. Add the confectioners' sugar and vanilla and mix well. Spread on the hot cake and cool on a wire rack.

Serves twelve to fifteen

CHOCOLATE CAKE

Cake

2	eggs
2	cups sugar
1/2	cup baking cocoa
2 1/2	cups flour
2	teaspoons baking soda
1	cup buttermilk
1 1/4	cups vegetable oil
1/8	teaspoon cream of tartar
1/2	teaspoon salt
1	cup very hot water

Chocolate Frosting

1/2	cup (1 stick) butter
6	tablespoons baking cocoa
1	(1-pound) package confectioners' sugar
2	tablespoons milk
2	teaspoons vanilla extract

To prepare the cake, combine the eggs, sugar, baking cocoa, flour, baking soda, buttermilk, vegetable oil, cream of tartar and salt in a large mixing bowl and beat at high speed until smooth. Add the hot water and beat for 1 minute longer.

Spoon the batter into 3 greased and floured 8-inch cake pans. Bake at 300 degrees for 30 to 40 minutes or until the layers test done. Cool in the pans for 5 minutes; then remove to a wire rack to cool completely.

To prepare the frosting, microwave the butter in a microwave-safe bowl until melted. Stir in the baking cocoa. Add the confectioners' sugar, milk and vanilla and stir until smooth. Spread between the layers and over the top and side of the cake.

Serves eight

The photograph for this recipe is on page 183.

CHOCOLATE TORTE

Chocolate Torte

1/2   cup (1 stick) butter
3   cups (18 ounces) semisweet chocolate chips
4   eggs
1/2   cup sugar
1   teaspoon vanilla extract

Vanilla Sauce

2   cups heavy cream
1/4   cup sugar
1/4   vanilla bean, split
4   egg yolks
1/4   cup sugar

Raspberry Sauce

1   (12-ounce) package frozen raspberries, thawed
2   to 4 tablespoons water
3   tablespoons sugar
2   tablespoons raspberry liqueur

To prepare the torte, butter a 9-inch springform pan and line the bottom and side with baking parchment. Melt 1/2 cup butter in a medium saucepan over low heat. Add the chocolate chips and heat until the chocolate melts, stirring constantly and taking care not to let burn. Remove from the heat.

Beat the eggs in a large bowl until fluffy. Add the sugar and vanilla and beat until the sugar dissolves. Stir several tablespoons of the warm chocolate into the egg mixture to temper; then stir in the remaining chocolate.

Spoon into the prepared springform pan. Bake at 325 degrees for 40 to 50 minutes or until the center begins to feel firm to the touch. Cool in the pan on a wire rack. Chill, covered, until serving time.

To prepare the vanilla sauce, combine the cream with 1/4 cup sugar in a medium saucepan. Scrape the seeds from the vanilla bean with a knife and add the seeds and the pod to the cream. Bring just to a boil over medium-low heat, stirring frequently. Remove from the heat; discard the vanilla bean pod.

Combine the egg yolks and 1/4 cup sugar in a medium bowl and whisk until smooth. Stir several tablespoons of the hot cream mixture into the egg yolks to temper; then stir the egg yolks into the remaining cream in the saucepan. Bring just to a boil, stirring frequently.

Pour into a medium bowl set into a larger bowl filled with ice, and stir for several minutes to cool. Chill, covered, until serving time.

To prepare the raspberry sauce, purée the raspberries in a blender. Add the water gradually, processing until the mixture is the desired consistency. Pour into a medium saucepan and add the sugar and raspberry liqueur. Bring to a boil over medium heat, stirring frequently. Spoon into a bowl and chill, covered, until serving time.

To serve, spoon some of the vanilla sauce and some of the raspberry sauce onto each serving plate. Remove the side of the springform pan and cut the torte into wedges. Invert a wedge into the sauces on each plate.

Serves twelve

HUMMINGBIRD CAKE

Cake

3	cups flour
2	cups sugar
1	teaspoon baking soda
1	teaspoon cinnamon
1	teaspoon salt
3	eggs, beaten
1 1/2	cups vegetable oil
1	(8-ounce) can crushed pineapple
2	cups chopped bananas, about 4 bananas
2	cups chopped pecans
1 1/2	teaspoons vanilla extract

Fluffy Cream Cheese Frosting

1	cup (2 sticks) butter or margarine, softened
16	ounces cream cheese, softened
2	(1-pound) packages confectioners' sugar
2	teaspoons vanilla extract
	salt to taste
1	cup chopped pecans

To prepare the cake, mix the flour, sugar, baking soda, cinnamon and salt in a large bowl. Add the eggs and vegetable oil and mix until moistened. Stir in the undrained pineapple, bananas, pecans and vanilla.

Spoon the batter into 3 greased and floured 9-inch cake pans. Bake at 350 degrees for 25 minutes or until a wooden pick comes out clean. Cool in the pans for 10 minutes; then remove to a wire rack to cool completely.

To prepare the frosting, beat the butter and cream cheese in a mixing bowl until light. Add the confectioners' sugar gradually and beat until fluffy. Stir in the vanilla and salt. Spread between the layers and over the top and side of the cake. Top with the pecans.

Serves eight to ten

DAZZLE YOUR GUESTS *by topping your cake with delicate and edible candied flowers. Sprinkle 2 envelopes of unflavored gelatin over 2 cups of water in a saucepan and let stand until softened. Heat until the gelatin dissolves, whisking constantly. Cool to room temperature. Dip edible flowers, such as pansies, into the gelatin mixture and shake to remove the excess. Sprinkle with superfine sugar, covering completely. Place on trays and let stand for 30 minutes or until firm and dry.*

ITALIAN CREAM CAKE

Cake

2	cups sugar
1/2	cup (1 stick) margarine, softened
1/2	cup vegetable oil
5	egg yolks
2	cups flour
1	teaspoon baking soda
1	cup buttermilk
1	teaspoon vanilla extract
1	cup flaked coconut
5	egg whites

Cream Cheese Pecan Frosting

1/2	cup (1 stick) margarine, softened
8	ounces cream cheese, softened
1	(1-pound) package confectioners' sugar
1	teaspoon vanilla extract
1	cup chopped pecans

To prepare the cake, combine the sugar, margarine and vegetable oil in a mixing bowl and beat until light. Beat in the egg yolks 1 at a time. Add the flour, baking soda, buttermilk, vanilla and coconut and mix well. Beat the egg whites in a mixing bowl until stiff peaks form. Fold into the cake batter.

Spoon the batter into 3 greased and floured 9-inch cake pans. Bake at 350 degrees for 25 minutes. Cool in the pans for 5 minutes; then remove to a wire rack to cool completely.

To prepare the frosting, combine the margarine and cream cheese in a mixing bowl and beat until light and fluffy. Add the confectioners' sugar, vanilla and pecans and mix well. Spread between the layers and over the top and side of the cake.

For the best results, do not use low-fat margarine or cream cheese for this cake.

Serves twelve

TEXAS WINE RECOMMENDATION: LA BUENA VIDA SPRINGTOWN MUSCAT DULCE

KAHLÚA CAKE

Cake

1	(2-layer) butter-recipe cake mix
1	(6-ounce) package chocolate instant pudding mix
4	eggs
1/2	cup sugar
1	cup vegetable oil
3/4	cup water
1/4	cup vodka
1/4	cup Kahlúa

Kahlúa Glaze

1	cup confectioners' sugar
2/3	cup Kahlúa

To prepare the cake, combine the cake mix and pudding mix in a mixing bowl. Add the eggs, sugar, vegetable oil, water, vodka and Kahlúa and mix just until moistened; do not overmix.

Spoon the batter into a greased and floured bundt pan. Bake at 350 degrees for 45 to 60 minutes or until the cake tests done. Cool in the pan for 10 minutes; then remove to a wire rack to cool while preparing the glaze.

To prepare the glaze, combine the confectioners' sugar with the Kahlúa in a bowl and mix until smooth. Drizzle over the warm cake.

Serves ten

KEY LIME CAKE

Cake

1	(2-layer) package lemon cake mix
1	(4-ounce) package lemon instant pudding mix
4	eggs
1	cup vegetable oil
3/4	cup water
1/4	cup Key lime juice

Key Lime Glaze and Garnish

2	cups confectioners' sugar
1/3	cup Key lime juice
2	tablespoons water
2	tablespoons melted butter
	confectioners' sugar
	sliced limes and strawberries

To prepare the cake, combine the cake mix and pudding mix in a mixing bowl. Add the eggs, vegetable oil, water and Key lime juice and beat at medium speed for 2 minutes.

Spoon the batter into a greased and floured 10-inch bundt pan. Bake at 350 degrees for 50 to 60 minutes or until a wooden pick inserted into the center comes out clean. Cool in the pan for 25 minutes; then invert onto a wire rack. Return the cake to the pan and pierce with a wooden pick or long-tined fork.

To prepare the glaze, combine 2 cups confectioners' sugar with the Key lime juice, water and melted butter in a medium mixing bowl and beat until smooth. Drizzle over the warm cake and let stand until completely cool. Invert onto a serving plate and dust with additional confectioners' sugar. Garnish with lime slices and strawberry slices.

Serves twelve to sixteen

CARAMEL POUND CAKE

3	tablespoons bread crumbs
3	cups flour
1	teaspoon baking powder
1/4	teaspoon salt
3/4	cup (1 1/2 sticks) butter, softened
2	cups packed light brown sugar
2	teaspoons vanilla extract
3	eggs
1	cup milk
2	tablespoons confectioners' sugar

Spray a 10-inch tube pan with nonstick cooking spray and coat with the bread crumbs. Combine the flour, baking powder and salt in a bowl and whisk to mix well. Cream the butter in a mixing bowl until light. Add the brown sugar and vanilla and beat until fluffy. Beat in the eggs 1 at a time. Add the flour mixture alternately with the milk, adding 1/2 of each at a time and beating until smooth after each addition.

Spoon the batter into the prepared tube pan. Bake at 350 degrees for 1 hour or until a wooden pick inserted in the center comes out clean. Cool in the pan for 10 minutes; then remove to a wire rack. Sift the confectioners' sugar over the cake and cool completely.
Serves twelve

IT IS IMPORTANT *to measure flour properly. It is rarely necessary to sift flour, but it is important to lighten the flour in the container before measuring by stirring with a wire whisk. Spoon the flour gently into a dry measuring cup and level the top with the straight edge of a knife. For a shortcut to measuring flour in a recipe that calls for sifting, decrease the amount of flour by 1 teaspoon per cup and whisk to lighten.*

CREAM CHEESE POUND CAKE

Cake

1¹/2   cups (3 sticks) butter, softened
4   ounces cream cheese, softened
1¹/2   cups sugar
3   eggs
1¹/2   cups flour
¹/8   teaspoon salt
1   teaspoon vanilla extract

Lemon Sauce

       grated zest and juice of 3 lemons
1   cup sugar
¹/2   cup (1 stick) butter
3   eggs, beaten

To prepare the cake, beat the butter and cream cheese at medium speed in a mixing bowl for 2 minutes or until light. Add the sugar gradually, beating for 5 to 7 minutes or until fluffy. Beat in the eggs 1 at a time at low speed. Add the flour, salt and vanilla and mix well.

Spoon the batter into 4 greased and floured miniature loaf pans. Place 2 cups of water in an oven preheated to 300 degrees. Bake the cake for 1 hour or until a wooden pick inserted into the centers comes out clean. Cool in the pans for 15 minutes; then remove to a wire rack to cool completely.

To prepare the sauce, combine the lemon zest, lemon juice, sugar and butter in a heavy medium saucepan. Cook over low heat until the butter melts, stirring to mix well. Whisk a small amount of the hot mixture into the eggs; then whisk the eggs into the hot mixture. Cook over low heat for 10 minutes or until thickened, stirring constantly; do not boil. Cool for 10 minutes and serve over the sliced cake.

Serves sixteen

TEXAS PRALINE CAKE

Cake

1 1/2 cups boiling water
1 cup rolled oats
1 cup sugar
1 cup packed brown sugar
1 cup vegetable oil
2 eggs
1 1/3 cups flour
1 teaspoon baking soda
1 teaspoon cinnamon
1/4 teaspoon salt

Pecan Topping

1/2 cup (1 stick) butter
2 tablespoons milk
1 cup packed brown sugar
1 cup chopped pecans

To prepare the cake, pour the boiling water over the oats in a bowl and let stand for several minutes. Combine the sugar, brown sugar, vegetable oil and eggs in a mixing bowl and beat until smooth. Add the flour, baking soda, cinnamon and salt and mix well. Stir in the oats mixture.

Spoon the batter into a greased 9×13-inch cake pan. Bake at 350 degrees for 30 minutes or until a wooden pick inserted in the center comes out clean.

To prepare the topping, combine the butter, milk and brown sugar in a saucepan and bring to a boil, stirring to mix well. Boil for 1 minute. Remove from the heat and stir in the pecans. Spread over the hot cake immediately.

You should not use instant oatmeal in this recipe.

Serves fifteen

PRALINE PUMPKIN TORTE

Torte

3/4 cup packed brown sugar
1/3 cup butter
3 tablespoons heavy cream
3/4 cup chopped pecans
2 cups flour
2 teaspoons baking powder
1 teaspoon baking soda
2 teaspoons pumpkin pie spice
1 teaspoon salt
4 eggs
1 2/3 cups sugar
1 cup vegetable oil
2 cups cooked or canned pumpkin
1/4 teaspoon vanilla extract

Torte Topping

1 3/4 cups whipping cream
1/4 cup confectioners' sugar
1/4 teaspoon vanilla extract
chopped pecans

To prepare the torte, combine the brown sugar, butter and cream in a heavy saucepan. Cook over low heat until the butter melts and the brown sugar dissolves, stirring to blend well. Pour into 2 greased 9-inch cake pans and sprinkle with the pecans. Let stand until cool.

Mix the flour, baking powder, baking soda, pumpkin pie spice and salt together. Combine the eggs, sugar and vegetable oil in a mixing bowl and beat until smooth. Add the pumpkin and vanilla and mix well. Add the dry ingredients and mix just until moistened.

Spoon the batter carefully into the prepared cake pans. Bake at 350 degrees for 30 to 35 minutes or until a wooden pick inserted in the center comes out clean. Cool in the pans for 5 minutes; then remove to a wire rack to cool completely.

To prepare the topping, beat the whipping cream until soft peaks form. Beat in the confectioners' sugar and vanilla.

To assemble, place 1 torte layer pecan side up on a cake plate and spread with 2/3 of the whipped cream mixture. Top with the remaining torte layer and whipped cream. Sprinkle with additional chopped pecans. Store in the refrigerator.

Serves twelve

CINDERELLA PUMPKIN CAKE

Cake

2	cups sugar
4	eggs
1	cup vegetable oil
2	cups flour
2	teaspoons baking soda
	cinnamon to taste
2	teaspoons salt
2	cups canned pumpkin

Creamy Frosting

3	ounces cream cheese, softened
1/2	cup (1 stick) butter, softened
1	(1-pound) package confectioners' sugar
1	teaspoon vanilla extract

To prepare the cake, combine the sugar and eggs in a mixing bowl and beat until pale yellow and thick. Beat in the vegetable oil. Add the flour, baking soda, cinnamon and salt and mix well. Stir in the pumpkin.

Spoon the batter into a greased bundt pan. Bake at 350 degrees for 45 to 55 minutes or until the cake tests done. Cool in the pan for 5 minutes; then remove to a wire rack to cool completely.

To prepare the frosting, combine the cream cheese and butter in a mixing bowl and beat until creamy. Add the confectioners' sugar and vanilla and mix until smooth. Spread over the cooled cake.

Serves twelve

PUMPKIN ROLL

Cake

3/4	cup sifted flour
1	teaspoon baking powder
2	teaspoons cinnamon
1/2	teaspoon ground nutmeg
1	teaspoon pumpkin pie spice
1/2	teaspoon salt
3	eggs
1	cup sugar
2/3	cup canned pumpkin
1	cup finely chopped walnuts
	confectioners' sugar

Cream Cheese Filling

8	ounces cream cheese, softened
6	tablespoons (3/4 stick) butter, softened
1	cup sifted confectioners' sugar
1	teaspoon vanilla extract

To prepare the cake, mix the flour, baking powder, cinnamon, nutmeg, pumpkin pie spice and salt together. Beat the eggs lightly in a mixing bowl. Add the sugar and beat until pale yellow and thick. Beat in the pumpkin. Stir in the flour mixture.

Spoon the batter into a 10×15-inch jelly roll pan lined with waxed paper. Sprinkle with the walnuts. Bake at 375 degrees for 15 minutes. Invert onto a towel sprinkled with confectioners' sugar and remove the waxed paper. Roll the cake from the narrow side in the towel and let stand until cool.

To prepare the filling, combine the cream cheese and butter in a mixing bowl and beat until smooth. Add the confectioners' sugar and vanilla and mix well.

To assemble, unroll the cake and spread with the filling. Reroll the cake to enclose the filling and place seam side down on a serving plate.
Serves ten

NEED HELP *rolling your next cake roll or jelly roll? Line the baking sheet with waxed paper before adding the batter. Sift confectioners' sugar onto a clean lint-free kitchen towel. When the cake is done, loosen the edges from the sides of the pan with a small knife and invert it onto the towel. Remove the waxed paper immediately and roll the cake in the towel, starting from the narrow side. Cool completely on a wire rack. Unroll the cake to spread it with the filling and roll again from the narrow side to enclose the filling. Place seam side down on a serving platter.*

TRES LECHES CAKE

2	cups sugar
8	egg yolks
2	cups flour
1	tablespoon baking powder
1/2	cup milk
1	tablespoon vanilla extract
8	egg whites
3	egg yolks
2	(12-ounce) cans evaporated milk
1	(14-ounce) can sweetened condensed milk
2	cups heavy cream
2	teaspoons vanilla extract
12	ounces whipped topping

Combine the sugar and 8 egg yolks in a mixing bowl and beat until pale yellow and thick. Add the flour, baking powder, milk and 1 tablespoon vanilla and beat until smooth. Beat the egg whites in a mixing bowl until very stiff peaks form. Fold very gently into the batter.

Spoon the batter into a greased and floured 9×13-inch cake pan. Bake at 350 degrees for 30 to 40 minutes or until the cake is light brown and tests done. Cool in the pan on a wire rack. Pierce holes in the cake.

Combine 3 egg yolks, the evaporated milk, sweetened condensed milk, cream and 2 teaspoons vanilla in a bowl and beat until smooth. Pour over the cake, allowing to soak in. Spread with the whipped topping.

This is best when prepared a day in advance. Store in the refrigerator after adding the whipped topping. To avoid uncooked egg yolks that may carry salmonella, you can use an equivalent amount of pasteurized egg yolk substitute.

Serves twelve

LECHE QUEMADA

1   (5-ounce) can evaporated milk
2   teaspoons light corn syrup
1   tablespoon butter
2   cups sugar
1   teaspoon butter
1/2 cup sugar
1   cup chopped pecans
1   teaspoon vanilla extract
     pinch of salt

Combine the evaporated milk with enough water to measure 1 cup. Combine with the corn syrup, 1 tablespoon butter and 2 cups sugar in a 2-quart saucepan and mix well. Heat until hot but not boiling. Add 1 teaspoon butter, 1/2 cup sugar, the pecans, vanilla and salt and mix well. Bring to a boil and cook for 10 minutes or to 240 degrees on a candy thermometer, soft-ball stage.

Remove from the heat and beat with a hand mixer or by hand until the mixture is lighter in color and thick enough not to spread when dropped from a spoon onto waxed paper. Drop onto the waxed paper and let stand until cool and firm. Store in an airtight container.

Do not overbeat the mixture, as it will become too hard and difficult to work with.
Makes three dozen

CHOCOLATE TOFFEE

1   (3-ounce) package slivered almonds
1   cup sugar
7/8 cup (1 3/4 sticks) butter
     salt to taste
6   chocolate candy bars

Spread the almonds in a single layer on a baking sheet lined with foil. Combine the sugar, butter and salt in a heavy saucepan. Cook over medium heat for 8 to 15 minutes or until the butter melts and the sugar dissolves, stirring to mix well. Cook to 270 to 290 degrees on a candy thermometer. Pour evenly over the almonds.

Arrange the candy bars over the hot mixture and let stand just until softened; spread evenly over the top. Let stand for 15 minutes. Cover with a sheet of foil and invert the entire mixture to place the chocolate on the bottom. Chill until firm and break into pieces. Store in an airtight container.
Serves six to eight

DOUBLE FUDGE BROWNIES

1¹/2   cups sugar
2/3   cup butter
¹/4   cup water
2   cups (12 ounces) semisweet chocolate chips
2   teaspoons vanilla extract
4   eggs
1¹/2   cups flour
¹/2   teaspoon baking soda
¹/2   teaspoon salt
1   cup chopped pecans
1¹/2   cups (9 ounces) semisweet chocolate chips

Combine the sugar, butter and water in a saucepan. Bring to a boil and remove from the heat; stir to mix well. Add 2 cups chocolate chips and vanilla and stir until the chocolate chips melt.

Transfer to a large mixing bowl and beat in the eggs 1 at a time. Add the flour, baking soda and salt and mix well. Stir in the pecans and 1¹/2 cups chocolate chips.

Spread in a greased 9×13-inch baking pan. Bake at 325 degrees for 40 minutes. Cool on a wire rack and cut into squares.

Makes two dozen

The photograph for this recipe is on page 16.

TEXANS *are close to the original source of chocolate, which was enjoyed by royalty and warriors in Latin America as an unsweetened ceremonial drink, sometimes flavored with chiles. It was introduced into Europe by Hernando Cortez. Europeans sweetened the drink and soon became literally addicted to it. It wasn't until the 19th century, however, that people realized that you could actually eat chocolate, and it came to be incorporated into desserts and confections of all kinds. It is still used to flavor savory dishes in Latin American cuisine, and Texans enjoy it both ways.*

FROSTED MOCHA BROWNIES

Crust

5	tablespoons butter, softened
1/3	cup packed brown sugar
2/3	cup flour
1/2	cup chopped pecans

Brownies

1/4	cup shortening
2	ounces unsweetened chocolate
1/4	cup (1/2 stick) butter
2	eggs
1/2	cup packed brown sugar
1	teaspoon vanilla extract
1/4	cup brewed strong coffee
1/2	cup flour
1/4	teaspoon salt
1/2	cup chopped pecans

Mocha Frosting

1/2	cup (1 stick) butter, softened
2	cups confectioners' sugar
1	tablespoon Kahlúa
2	tablespoons heavy cream
	milk

Topping

3	tablespoons butter
4	ounces semisweet chocolate
1/4	cup confectioners' sugar

To prepare the crust, cream 5 tablespoons butter with 1/3 cup brown sugar in a mixing bowl until light and fluffy. Add 2/3 cup flour and mix well. Mix in 1/2 cup pecans. Press the mixture over the bottom of a greased 9×9-inch baking pan.

To prepare the brownies, combine the shortening, chocolate and 1/4 cup butter in a saucepan. Melt over low heat, stirring to blend well. Remove from the heat and cool. Combine the eggs, 1/2 cup brown sugar and vanilla in a large bowl and beat until smooth. Add the chocolate mixture and mix well. Stir in the coffee, 1/2 cup flour, salt and 1/2 cup pecans.

Spread the batter in the prepared baking pan. Bake at 350 degrees for 25 minutes or until a wooden pick inserted in the center comes out clean. Cool on a wire rack.

To prepare the frosting, cream 1/2 cup butter and 2 cups confectioners' sugar in a mixing bowl until light and fluffy. Add the liqueur and cream and mix until smooth, adding a small amount of milk if necessary for spreading consistency. Spread over the baked layer.

To prepare the topping, melt 3 tablespoons butter and the semisweet chocolate in a saucepan over low heat. Stir in 1/4 cup confectioners' sugar. Spread over the top. Let stand until firm. Cut into 1 1/2-inch squares to serve.

Makes three dozen

PEPPERMINT PATTY BROWNIES

Brownies

1/2	cup (1 stick) butter
3	ounces unsweetened baking chocolate
2	eggs
1	cup sugar
3/4	cup flour
1/4	teaspoon baking soda
1	teaspoon vanilla extract
10	chocolate-covered peppermint patties, cut into quarters

Chocolate Glaze

1/4	cup semisweet chocolate chips
2	tablespoons butter
1	tablespoon corn syrup

To prepare the brownies, heat the butter and chocolate in a 2-quart saucepan over medium heat for 4 to 6 minutes or until melted, stirring to blend well. Combine the eggs and sugar in a mixing bowl and beat until pale yellow and thick. Add the flour, baking soda and vanilla and mix well. Add the chocolate mixture and mix until smooth.

Spread half the batter in an 8×8-inch baking pan which has been greased on the bottom only. Arrange the peppermint patties carefully over the batter and top with the remaining batter. Bake at 350 degrees for 25 to 27 minutes or until the brownies begin to pull away from the sides of the pan. Cool on a wire rack for 30 minutes or longer.

To prepare the glaze, melt the chocolate chips and butter in a 1-quart saucepan over low heat, stirring until smooth. Stir in the corn syrup. Let stand for 10 minutes or until the mixture begins to thicken. Spread over the cooled brownies. Chill, covered, for 10 minutes or until the glaze sets. Cut into small squares.

Makes twenty-five

GINGER CRACKLE COOKIES

2¹/4   cups flour
2   teaspoons baking soda
1   teaspoon cinnamon
1   teaspoon ginger
³/4   teaspoon cloves
¹/4   teaspoon salt
³/4   cup shortening
1   cup sugar
1   egg
¹/4   cup dark molasses
     sugar

Mix the flour, baking soda, cinnamon, ginger, cloves and salt together. Cream the shortening and 1 cup sugar in a mixing bowl until light and fluffy. Add the egg and molasses and mix until smooth. Add the flour mixture and mix well. Chill in the refrigerator for 1 hour.

Shape the dough into 1-inch balls and roll in additional sugar. Place 2 inches apart on an ungreased cookie sheet. Bake at 375 degrees for 10 minutes or until the cookies are light brown and the tops crackle. Cool on the cookie sheet.
Makes four dozen

MERINGUES

4   egg whites
¹/8   teaspoon cream of tartar
¹/4   teaspoon salt
1   teaspoon vanilla extract
1¹/2   cups sugar
2   cups (12 ounces) miniature chocolate chips

Combine the egg whites, cream of tartar, salt and vanilla in a mixing bowl and beat until stiff peaks form. Add the sugar gradually, beating constantly. Fold in the chocolate chips. Drop onto a cookie sheet lined with brown paper. Bake at 300 degrees for 20 minutes or until the peaks are light brown. Cool on the cookie sheet. Remove from the brown paper and store in an airtight container.
Makes two dozen

OATMEAL TOFFEE COOKIES

1¹/2	cups flour
1	teaspoon baking soda
1	cup (2 sticks) unsalted butter, softened
³/4	cup sugar
³/4	cup packed brown sugar
1	egg
1	teaspoon vanilla extract
1¹/2	cups rolled oats
1	cup dried cherries
1	cup (6 ounces) chopped bittersweet chocolate
1	cup (6 ounces) toffee chips

Sift the flour and baking soda together. Combine the butter, sugar and brown sugar in a mixing bowl and beat at medium speed with the paddle attachment for 2 to 3 minutes or until light and fluffy, scraping down the sides of the bowl several times. Add the egg and beat at high speed until smooth. Beat in the vanilla. Add the flour mixture gradually, mixing constantly at low speed. Mix in the oats, cherries, chocolate and toffee chips at low speed.

Divide the dough into 3 portions and roll each portion in plastic wrap to form logs 1¹/2 inches in diameter. Cut the logs into ³/4-inch slices and arrange on baking parchment-lined cookie sheets. Bake at 350 degrees for 8 to10 minutes or until golden brown. Remove to a wire rack to cool.

Makes three dozen

WALNUT CRESCENT COOKIES

1	cup (2 sticks) butter, softened
2	cups confectioners' sugar
1¹/2	teaspoons water
2	cups flour
2	teaspoons vanilla extract
1	cup finely chopped walnuts
	confectioners' sugar

Cream the butter in a mixing bowl until light. Add ¹/4 cup of the confectioners' sugar and beat until fluffy. Add the remaining 1³/4 cups confectioners' sugar, water, flour, vanilla and walnuts and mix well. Shape into logs ¹/2 inch in diameter and cut into 1-inch pieces.

Place the dough on a cookie sheet and shape into crescents. Bake at 375 degrees for 15 minutes. Roll the warm cookies in additional confectioners' sugar and cool on a wire rack. Roll again in the confectioners' sugar when cool.

Makes six dozen

PEAR CUSTARD BARS

Crust

1/2 cup (1 stick) butter or margarine, softened
1/3 cup sugar
3/4 cup flour
1/4 teaspoon vanilla extract
2/3 cup chopped macadamias

Pear Filling

8   ounces cream cheese, softened
1/2 cup sugar
1   egg
1/2 teaspoon vanilla extract
1   (15-ounce) can pear halves, drained
1/2 teaspoon sugar
1/2 teaspoon cinnamon

To prepare the crust, cream the butter and sugar in a mixing bowl until light and fluffy. Add the flour and vanilla and mix well. Stir in the macadamias. Press into a greased 8×8-inch baking pan. Bake at 350 degrees for 20 minutes or until light brown. Cool on a wire rack. Increase the oven temperature to 375 degrees.

To prepare the filling, beat the cream cheese in a mixing bowl until light. Add 1/2 cup sugar, the egg and vanilla and beat until smooth. Spoon over the crust. Cut the pears into 1/8-inch slices and arrange in a single layer over the filling. Sprinkle with a mixture of 1/2 teaspoon sugar and the cinnamon.

Bake at 375 degrees for 28 to 30 minutes or until set. Cool on a wire rack for 45 minutes. Chill, covered, for 2 hours or longer before cutting into bars. Store in the refrigerator.
Serves sixteen

THE RICH SOIL *of Collin County's Blackland Prairie has provided the perfect environment for the growth of many wild fruits. Early settlers of the area enjoyed the sweet flavor of grapes, persimmons, plums, and dewberries. Dewberries, a relative of the blackberry, were savored in juicy cobblers, perhaps at the Old Settlers Picnic often held in July, the peak of dewberry season.*

RANGER COOKIES

5	cups rolled oats
4	cups flour
2	teaspoons baking powder
2	teaspoons baking soda
1	teaspoon salt
2	cups (4 sticks) butter, softened
2	cups sugar
2	cups packed brown sugar
4	eggs
2	teaspoons vanilla extract
4	cups (24 ounces) chocolate chips
1	(8-ounce) chocolate candy bar, grated
3	cups chopped nuts

Process the oats in a blender until finely chopped. Mix with the flour, baking powder, baking soda and salt. Cream the butter, sugar and brown sugar in a mixing bowl until light and fluffy. Beat in the eggs and vanilla. Add the dry ingredients and mix well. Stir in the chocolate chips, grated chocolate and nuts.

Shape the dough into balls and arrange 2 inches apart on cookie sheets. Bake at 375 degrees for 10 minutes. Remove to a wire rack to cool.

Makes nine dozen

SUGAR COOKIES

4^{1}/$_{4}$	cups flour
1	teaspoon baking soda
1	teaspoon cream of tartar
1	teaspoon salt
1	cup (2 sticks) butter, softened
^{3}/$_{4}$	cup vegetable oil
1	cup sugar
1	cup confectioners' sugar
2	eggs
1	tablespoon vanilla extract
	sugar

Mix the flour, baking soda, cream of tartar and salt together. Combine the butter, vegetable oil, 1 cup sugar and confectioners' sugar in a mixing bowl and beat until smooth. Beat the eggs with the vanilla in a small bowl. Add to the sugar mixture and mix well. Add the dry ingredients and mix to form a dough. Chill for 8 hours or longer.

Shape the dough into small balls and place on a cookie sheet. Press with a glass or cookie press dipped in additional sugar. Bake at 375 degrees for 12 to 15 minutes or until golden brown. Remove to a wire rack to cool.

Makes three dozen

FROSTED SUGAR COOKIES

Cookies

1   cup (2 sticks) butter, softened
1   cup sugar
1   egg
1   teaspoon vanilla extract
1/2   teaspoon almond extract (optional)
2   teaspoons baking powder
3   cups flour

Royal Frosting

3   tablespoons meringue powder
4   cups confectioners' sugar
5   to 6 tablespoons water
        food coloring (optional)

To prepare the cookies, cream the butter and sugar in a mixing bowl until light and fluffy. Beat in the egg. Add the flavorings and baking powder and mix until smooth. Stir in the flour 1 cup at a time, mixing to form a dough.

Roll 1/4 inch thick on a lightly floured surface. Cut into desired shapes with cookie cutters. Arrange on an ungreased cookie sheet. Bake at 400 degrees for 10 minutes or until the edges are light brown. Remove to a wire rack to cool.

To prepare the frosting, mix the meringue powder and confectioners' sugar in a mixing bowl. Add enough water to make of spreading consistency and beat until smooth. Add food coloring if desired. Spread on the cooled cookies.

Makes three dozen

TEXAS WINE RECOMMENDATION: CAP ROCK WINERY SPARKLING WINE

The photograph for this recipe is on page 11.

SUBSTITUTE *Butter Frosting for Royal Frosting on sugar cookies or other cookies. Combine a 1-pound package of confectioners' sugar with 1 stick of softened butter and 1 tablespoon vanilla or almond extract in a bowl. Add 2 to 3 tablespoons milk, or as much as needed for spreading consistency, and beat until smooth.*

APPLE CHEESE TORTE

Torte Crust

1	cup (2 sticks) butter, softened
2/3	cup sugar
2	cups flour
1/2	teaspoon vanilla extract

Filling

8	ounces cream cheese, softened
1/4	cup sugar
1	egg
1	teaspoon vanilla extract
5	or 6 Granny Smith apples, peeled and thinly sliced
1	tablespoon lemon juice
1/3	cup sugar
1	teaspoon cinnamon
1/4	cup sliced almonds

To prepare the crust, cream the butter and sugar in a mixing bowl until light and fluffy. Add the flour and vanilla and mix well. Press over the bottom and 3/4 up the side of a greased 8- or 9-inch springform pan.

To prepare the filling, combine the cream cheese, 1/4 cup sugar, egg and vanilla in a mixing bowl and beat until smooth. Spoon over the crust. Toss the apples with the lemon juice, 1/3 cup sugar and cinnamon in a bowl. Spread over the cheese mixture and sprinkle with the almonds. Press the crust mixture down even with the filling using a spoon.

Bake at 450 degrees for 10 minutes. Reduce the oven temperature to 400 degrees and bake for 25 minutes longer. Serve warm or cool. Store in the refrigerator.
Serves eight

ADOBE APPLE PIE

Pastry

3/4	cup shortening
2	cups flour
1	teaspoon salt
6	to 7 tablespoons cold water

Filling

1	pound apples, peeled and sliced, or 1 (16-ounce) can sliced apples
2	tablespoons fresh lemon juice
1/2	teaspoon nutmeg
1/2	teaspoon cinnamon
1/2	cup sugar
1/4	cup seedless raisins
1	cup packed brown sugar
2	tablespoons flour
2	tablespoons butter
1/2	cup chopped pecans
4	tablespoons milk

Hard Sauce

1/2	cup (1 stick) butter, softened
1 1/2	cups confectioners' sugar
1	tablespoon boiling water
1	teaspoon brandy or rum

To prepare the pastry, combine the shortening, flour and salt in a bowl and work with the fingers until crumbly. Add enough water to bind the dough. Divide into 2 equal portions and shape into balls. Roll 1 portion into a circle on a lightly floured pastry cloth and fit into a 9-inch pie pan. Roll the second portion to fit the top.

To prepare the filling, arrange the apples in the prepared pie pan and sprinkle with the lemon juice, nutmeg and cinnamon, then with the sugar and raisins. Combine the brown sugar, flour and butter in a bowl and mix until crumbly. Sprinkle over the apples and top with the pecans. Drizzle with 3 tablespoons of the milk.

Place the top pastry over the filling. Seal and trim the edges and prick with a fork. Brush with the remaining 1 tablespoon milk. Bake at 450 degrees for 10 minutes. Reduce the oven temperature to 350 degrees and bake for 30 minutes longer or until the crust is golden brown.

To prepare the hard sauce, cream the butter in a mixing bowl until light. Add the confectioners' sugar and beat until fluffy. Beat in the boiling water and brandy. Serve on the pie.

Serves eight

BLUEBERRY PEACH PIE

Almond Pastry

1 1/4   cups flour
1   teaspoon sugar
1/2   cup coarsely chopped slivered almonds
1/3   cup vegetable oil
3   to 4 tablespoons water

Filling

1   cup sugar
3   tablespoons cornstarch
1   cup water
1/4   cup lemon gelatin
4   cups peeled and sliced fresh peaches
3/4   cup fresh blueberries
       sweetened whipped cream
       mint sprigs

To prepare the pastry, combine the flour, sugar, almonds and vegetable oil in a medium bowl. Add the water gradually, mixing until evenly moistened. Press the mixture into a 9-inch pie plate. Bake at 375 degrees for 20 minutes. Cool on a wire rack.

To prepare the filling, combine the sugar, cornstarch and water in a saucepan. Bring to a boil over medium heat. Cook for 1 minute, stirring constantly. Remove from the heat. Add the gelatin and mix to dissolve completely.

Mix the peaches and blueberries in a large bowl. Add the gelatin mixture and toss gently. Spoon into the pie shell and cover with plastic wrap or foil. Chill for 1 hour. Serve chilled with a dollop of sweetened whipped cream and a sprig of mint.

Serves eight

PECAN TREES, *the official state tree of Texas, grow wild along almost every river and stream in the state. In fact, they were so plentiful that the early pioneers of Plano enjoyed native pecans by the bushel. Texas leads the nation as the largest producer of native pecans, which are known for their high oil content and added flavor. Today these trees are prized not only for their pecans, but also for their wood, which is used to make furniture and baseball bats.*

CRANBERRY PIE

2	cups fresh cranberries
1/2	cup sugar
1/2	cup coarsely chopped pecans
1	unbaked (9-inch) pie shell
1/4	cup (1/2 stick) margarine
2	tablespoons shortening
1	egg
1/2	cup sugar
1/2	cup flour

Combine the cranberries, 1/2 cup sugar and pecans in a bowl. Spoon into the pie shell. Melt the margarine and shortening in a small saucepan and mix well. Add the egg, 1/2 cup sugar and flour and mix well. Spread over the cranberry mixture. Bake at 325 degrees for 45 minutes.

You should increase the oven temperature to 350 degrees if using a metal pie plate.

Serves eight

TEXAS WINE RECOMMENDATION: BRUSHY CREEK VINEYARDS TEXAS PORT

FUDGE PECAN PIE

6	tablespoons unsweetened baking cocoa
6	tablespoons flour
1 1/2	cups sugar
3	eggs, beaten
1 1/2	teaspoons vanilla extract
3/4	cup (1 1/2 sticks) unsalted butter, melted
3/4	cup chopped pecans
1	unbaked (9-inch) pie shell

Sift the baking cocoa, flour and sugar into a bowl. Add the eggs and vanilla and mix well. Blend in the butter. Stir in the pecans. Spoon into the pie shell. Bake at 350 degrees for 30 to 35 minutes or until the top is crusty. Serve with ice cream.

Serves six to eight

HONEY CRUNCH PECAN PIE

Pie

4	eggs, lightly beaten
1	cup light corn syrup
1/4	cup sugar
1/4	cup packed brown sugar
2	tablespoons butter, melted
1	teaspoon vanilla extract
1/2	teaspoon salt
1	cup chopped pecans
1	unbaked deep-dish pie shell

Crunch Topping

1/3	cup plus 1 tablespoon packed brown sugar
1/4	cup honey
1/4	cup (1/2 stick) butter
2	cups pecan halves

To prepare the pie, combine the eggs, corn syrup, sugar, brown sugar, butter, vanilla and salt in a mixing bowl and beat until smooth. Stir in the pecans. Spoon into the pie shell. Bake at 350 degrees for 40 minutes.

To prepare the topping, combine the brown sugar, honey and butter in a medium saucepan. Cook over medium heat for 2 to 3 minutes or until the butter melts and the sugar dissolves, stirring to mix well. Stir in the pecan halves. Spread over the pie.

Bake the pie for 10 to 15 minutes longer or until the topping is golden brown.

Serves six to eight

MERINGUE CRUST LEMON CREAM PIE

Meringue Crust

4	egg whites, at room temperature
1	tablespoon cold water
1/2	teaspoon cream of tartar
1	cup sugar

Filling and Topping

4	egg yolks
1/2	cup sugar
3	tablespoons fresh lemon juice
1 1/2	teaspoons grated lemon zest
2	cups whipping cream
2	to 3 tablespoons confectioners' sugar
1	teaspoon vanilla extract

To prepare the crust, beat the egg whites with the cold water in a small mixing bowl until foamy. Add the cream of tartar and beat for 3 minutes or until the mixture thickens. Transfer to a large bowl. Add the sugar gradually, beating constantly at high speed until glossy peaks form. Spread in a lightly greased 9-inch pie plate, shaping to form a crust. Bake at 300 degrees for 40 minutes. Turn off the oven and let stand in the oven until cool.

To prepare the filling and topping, beat the egg yolks in a mixing bowl until pale yellow and thick. Add the sugar, lemon juice and lemon zest and mix well. Transfer to a double boiler and cook for 10 minutes or until thickened, stirring constantly. Beat 1 cup of the whipping cream in a mixing bowl until stiff peaks form. Fold into the lemon mixture. Spoon into the meringue crust.

Combine the remaining cup of whipping cream with the confectioners' sugar and vanilla in a mixing bowl and beat until soft peaks form. Spread over the filling. Chill until serving time.
Serves eight

PEACHES AND CREAM PIE

No-Roll Pastry

3/4	cup flour
1	(4-ounce) package vanilla instant pudding mix
1/2	teaspoon baking powder
3	tablespoons butter, melted
1	egg, beaten
1/4	to 1/2 cup milk

Filling

1	(29-ounce) can sliced peaches
8	ounces cream cheese, softened
1/2	cup sugar
1	to 3 tablespoons cinnamon sugar, or to taste

To prepare the pastry, mix the flour, pudding mix and baking powder in a mixing bowl. Add the butter and egg. Add the milk gradually, adding just enough to form a dough. Press the dough into a lightly buttered 10-inch pie pan with moistened fingers.

To prepare the filling, drain the peaches, reserving 3 tablespoons of the juice. Spread the peaches in the prepared pie pan. Combine the reserved peach juice with the cream cheese and sugar in a mixing bowl and beat until smooth. Spread over the peaches. Sprinkle with cinnamon sugar.

Bake the pie at 350 degrees for 40 to 50 minutes or until set. Cool on a wire rack. Store, covered, in the refrigerator.

Serves six to eight

JUICY TEXAS PEACHES *ripened in the sun have a cream to yellow background with a bright red blush; it's your assurance that you are buying the sweetest peach available. To remove the skin from a peach, you can drop it into boiling water for about one minute; then remove it to an ice bath. The skin should slip right off the peach.*

CRÈME BRÛLÉE

1	vanilla bean, or 1 tablespoon vanilla extract
4	cups heavy cream
	pinch of salt
8	egg yolks
3/4	cup sugar
1/2	cup packed light brown sugar

Split the vanilla bean and scrape the seeds into the cream in a medium saucepan. Add the vanilla pod and the salt and heat until warm. Beat the egg yolks with the sugar in a large mixing bowl until pale yellow and thick. Remove the vanilla pod from the cream and add the cream to the egg mixture gradually, mixing well.

Spoon into 6 ramekins and place the ramekins in a shallow baking pan filled with 1 inch hot water. Bake at 300 degrees for 40 minutes. Remove to a wire rack and cool for 30 minutes. Sift the brown sugar over the custards and place on a baking sheet. Broil for 15 seconds or just until the brown sugar melts and forms a firm glaze.
Serves six

TEXAS WINE RECOMMENDATION: TEXAS HILLS MOSCATO

RUM CHOCOLATE MOUSSE

1/4	cup sugar
2	to 4 tablespoons rum
4	ounces semisweet chocolate or milk chocolate
2	to 3 tablespoons whipping cream
2	egg whites
2	cups whipped cream
	chocolate-covered almonds
	sweetened whipped cream and shaved chocolate

Combine the sugar and rum in a saucepan and cook over very low heat, stirring until the sugar is dissolved but not brown. Melt the chocolate in a double boiler. Remove the double boiler from the heat and stir 2 to 3 tablespoons cream into the chocolate. Add the rum mixture and mix until smooth. Cool to room temperature.

Beat the egg whites in a mixing bowl until stiff peaks form. Fold into the chocolate mixture. Fold in the whipped cream gently.

Spoon into dessert glasses and chill for 2 hours or longer. Garnish with chocolate-covered almonds or a dollop of additional sweetened whipped cream and shaved chocolate.

To avoid uncooked egg whites that may carry salmonella, you can use an equivalent amount of pasteurized egg white substitute.
Serves eight to ten

LEMON DELIGHT

Pecan Crust

1 1/2   cups vanilla wafer crumbs
1/2   cup chopped pecans
1/4   cup (1/2 stick) butter, melted
2   tablespoons sugar

Filling

1/2   gallon vanilla ice cream
3   tablespoons lemon juice
1   teaspoon grated lemon zest
3/4   cup sugar
4 1/2   tablespoons butter
1   egg
1   egg yolk
1   cup whipping cream
1   tablespoon sugar

To prepare the crust, mix the vanilla wafer crumbs, pecans, butter and sugar in a bowl. Press over the bottom of a 9×13-inch baking pan. Bake at 350 degrees for 10 minutes. Cool on a wire rack.

To prepare the filling, soften the ice cream at room temperature until spreading consistency. Spread over the cooled crust. Freeze until firm.

Combine the lemon juice, lemon zest, 3/4 cup sugar, butter, egg and egg yolk in a saucepan and mix well. Cook over low heat until thickened and smooth, stirring constantly. Cool to room temperature. Spread over the ice cream. Freeze until firm.

Combine the whipping cream and 1 tablespoon sugar in a mixing bowl and beat until soft peaks form. Spread over the lemon layer. Freeze for 8 hours or longer before serving.
Serves twelve

POACHED PEARS WITH RASPBERRY SAUCE

Pears

2	cups sugar
1	cup dry white wine
4 1/2	cups water
	grated zest and juice of 2 lemons
2	teaspoons vanilla extract
6	large Bosc or Bartlett pears

Raspberry Sauce

2	cups raspberries
1/2	to 1 cup confectioners' sugar
2	tablespoons (about) orange juice

To prepare the pears, combine the sugar, wine and water in a saucepan large enough to hold 6 pears and cover them completely with the liquid. Add the lemon zest, lemon juice and vanilla and mix well. Bring to a boil and cook for 2 to 3 minutes or until the sugar dissolves, stirring frequently. Remove from the heat.

Slice just enough from the bottom of each pear to enable it to stand upright. Peel the pears, leaving the stem and any leaves intact. Arrange in the hot syrup in the saucepan; the liquid should cover the pears. Cover the saucepan and bring to a boil. Cook for 30 minutes or until the pears are fork-tender. Remove from the heat and cool in the syrup for 3 hours.

To prepare the sauce, purée the raspberries in a blender or food processor. Press through a sieve into a bowl to remove the seeds. Add enough confectioners' sugar to sweeten to taste. Add enough orange juice to make of the desired consistency and mix well. Spoon the sauce onto serving plates and place a pear in the sauce on each plate.
Serves six

The photographs for this recipe are on pages 22 and 23.

CHOCOLATE-GLAZED TRIPLE-LAYER CHEESECAKE

Chocolate Crust

9	ounces chocolate wafer cookies, crushed
1/4	cup sugar
5	tablespoons butter, melted

Triple-Layer Filling

8	ounces cream cheese, softened
1/4	cup sugar
1	egg
1/4	teaspoon vanilla extract
2	ounces semisweet chocolate, melted
1/3	cup sour cream
8	ounces cream cheese, softened
1/3	cup packed dark brown sugar
1	tablespoon flour
1	egg
1/2	teaspoon vanilla extract
1/4	cup chopped pecans
5	ounces cream cheese, softened
1/4	cup sugar
1	egg
1	cup (8 ounces) sour cream
1/4	teaspoon vanilla extract
1/4	teaspoon almond extract

Chocolate Glaze

6	ounces semisweet chocolate
1/4	cup (1/2 stick) butter
3/4	cup sifted confectioners' sugar
2	tablespoons hot water
1	teaspoon vanilla extract

To prepare the crust, combine the chocolate cookie crumbs, sugar and butter in a bowl and mix well. Press over the bottom of an 8- or 9-inch springform pan.

To prepare the filling, combine 8 ounces cream cheese and 1/4 cup sugar in a mixing bowl and beat until smooth. Beat in 1 egg and 1/4 teaspoon vanilla. Stir in the melted chocolate and 1/3 cup sour cream. Spread evenly in the prepared springform pan.

Combine 8 ounces cream cheese with the brown sugar and flour in a mixing bowl and beat until smooth. Beat in 1 egg and 1/2 teaspoon vanilla. Stir in the pecans. Spread evenly over the chocolate layer. Combine 5 ounces cream cheese with 1/4 cup sugar in a mixing bowl and beat until smooth. Beat in 1 egg. Stir in 1 cup sour cream, 1/4 teaspoon vanilla and the almond extract. Spread evenly over the pecan layer. Bake at 325 degrees for 1 hour. Turn off the oven and let the cheesecake stand in the closed oven for 30 minutes. Open the oven door and let stand for 30 minutes longer. Cool completely on a wire rack. Cover and chill for 8 hours. Place on a serving plate and remove the side of the springform pan.

To prepare the glaze, melt the chocolate and butter in a small saucepan, stirring to blend well. Add the confectioners' sugar, hot water and vanilla and mix well. Spread the warm glaze over the chilled cheesecake. Cool to room temperature and chill until serving time.

Serves ten to twelve

MOCHA CHEESECAKE

Chocolate Pecan Crust

1¹/2	cups chocolate cookie crumbs
1¹/2	cups ground toasted pecans
6	tablespoons (³/4 stick) butter, melted
4	ounces semisweet chocolate, melted

Filling

16	ounces cream cheese, softened
1	cup packed brown sugar
4	eggs
2	teaspoons vanilla extract
8	ounces semisweet chocolate, melted
¹/3	cup brewed strong coffee
1	cup (8 ounces) sour cream

Chocolate Glaze

4	ounces semisweet chocolate chips
¹/3	cup heavy cream
2	tablespoons sugar

To prepare the crust, combine the chocolate cookie crumbs, pecans and butter in a bowl and mix well. Press over the bottom and side of a 9-inch springform pan. Drizzle with the melted chocolate. Chill until the chocolate is firm.

To prepare the filling, combine the cream cheese and brown sugar in a mixing bowl and beat until fluffy. Add the eggs 1 at a time, beating for 1 minute after each addition. Beat in the vanilla and melted chocolate. Add the coffee, and then the sour cream, mixing well.

Spoon into the prepared springform pan. Place in a 300-degree oven and place a pan of water on a lower oven rack. Bake for 1 hour. Reduce the oven temperature to 275 degrees and bake for 1 hour. Reduce the oven temperature to 250 degrees and bake for 30 minutes longer. Turn off the oven and let stand in the oven with the oven door ajar for 30 minutes. Chill in the refrigerator for 4 hours.

To prepare the glaze, melt the chocolate chips in a saucepan. Add the cream and sugar and mix well. Cool to lukewarm. Pour over the cheesecake. Chill for 1 hour or until set.

Place the cheesecake on a serving plate and remove the side of the springform pan.

Serves twelve

SUNSHINE CHEESECAKE

Graham Cracker Crust

1	cup graham cracker crumbs
3	tablespoons sugar
3	tablespoons butter, melted

Filling

24	ounces cream cheese, softened
1	cup sugar
3	tablespoons flour
2	tablespoons lemon juice
1	tablespoon grated lemon zest
1/2	teaspoon vanilla extract
3	eggs
1	egg white

Lemon Glaze and Garnish

3/4	cup sugar
2	tablespoons cornstarch
1/2	cup cold water
1/4	cup lemon juice
1	egg yolk, beaten
	sugared lemon or orange slices

To prepare the crust, mix the graham cracker crumbs, sugar and butter in a bowl. Press over the bottom of a 9-inch springform pan. Bake at 325 degrees for 10 minutes.

To prepare the filling, combine the cream cheese, sugar, flour, lemon juice, lemon zest and vanilla in a mixing bowl and beat until smooth. Beat in the eggs and egg white 1 at a time.

Spoon into the prepared crust. Bake at 450 degrees for 10 minutes. Reduce the oven temperature to 250 degrees and bake for 30 minutes longer. Remove to a wire rack and loosen the edge of the pan with a knife. Let stand until cool.

To prepare the glaze, combine the sugar, cornstarch, water and lemon juice in a saucepan and mix well. Cook over medium-high heat until thickened and clear, stirring constantly. Stir a small amount of the hot mixture into the egg yolk; then stir the egg yolk into the hot mixture. Cook over medium to low heat for 3 minutes longer, stirring constantly. Cool slightly and spoon over the cheesecake.

Place on a serving plate and remove the side of the pan. Garnish with sugared lemon or orange slices. Cut by pressing dental floss through the cheesecake and pulling out the side at the bottom.

Serves twelve

TURTLE CHEESECAKE

Crumb Crust

2   cups vanilla wafer crumbs
6   tablespoons (3/4 stick) butter, melted

Filling

1   (14-ounce) package caramels
1   (5-ounce) can evaporated milk
1   cup chopped pecans
16   ounces cream cheese, softened
1/2   cup sugar
1   teaspoon vanilla extract
2   eggs
1/2   cup (3 ounces) semisweet chocolate chips

To prepare the crust, mix the vanilla wafer crumbs and butter in a bowl. Press over the bottom and side of a springform pan. Bake at 350 degrees for 10 minutes.

To prepare the filling, melt the caramels with the evaporated milk in a saucepan over low heat, stirring to blend well. Spread over the baked crust and sprinkle with the pecans. Combine the cream cheese, sugar and vanilla in a mixing bowl and beat until smooth. Beat in the eggs 1 at a time. Stir in the chocolate chips. Spoon into the prepared springform pan.

Bake at 350 degrees for 40 minutes. Place on a wire rack to cool. Chill in the refrigerator. Place on a serving plate and remove the side of the springform pan to serve.
Serves twelve

TEXAS WINE RECOMMENDATION: HIDDEN SPRINGS WINERY MUSCAT CANELLI

A WATER BATH *can prevent your cheesecake from cracking. Place the cheesecake pan in a similarly shaped larger pan and add hot water to reach 2/3 of the way up the side of the cheesecake pan. You can also place a towel in the bottom of the larger pan to prevent sloshing and to insulate. If you continue to have trouble with cracking, add 1 tablespoon of cornstarch to the batter. If you are using a springform pan, be sure to line the outside with foil to prevent leaking.*

HAZELNUT FUDGE ICE CREAM

1   quart heavy cream
1   quart half-and-half
1   quart milk
1   (14-ounce) can sweetened condensed milk
1   cup sugar
3/4 cup Nutella
2   tablespoons hazelnut syrup

Combine the cream, half-and-half, milk and sweetened condensed milk in a large bowl and mix well. Add the sugar, Nutella and hazelnut syrup and mix until smooth. Pour into the ice cream freezer container and freeze using the manufacturer's instructions.
Serves sixteen

LIME ICE CREAM WITH BERRIES

1   cup sugar
2   cups heavy cream
1/2 cup lime juice, from about 4 limes
2   teaspoons grated lime zest
6   sugar cookie cups
3   cups seasonal berries

Combine the sugar and cream in a mixing bowl and beat until the sugar dissolves. Add the lime juice and lime zest. Pour into a 1-quart ice cream freezer container and freeze using the manufacturer's instructions. Fill the sugar cookie cups with the berries and top with the ice cream.

You may substitute the juice of other citrus fruits for the lime juice if preferred.
Serves six

PIÑA COLADA ICE CREAM

2   (15-ounce) cans cream of coconut
1   (16-ounce) can crushed pineapple, drained
1   teaspoon vanilla extract
1   cup chopped pecans
1/2 cup coconut (optional)
2   cups (about) milk

Combine the cream of coconut, pineapple and vanilla in a bowl and mix well. Stir in the pecans and coconut. Spoon into an ice cream freezer container and add milk to the fill line. Freeze using the manufacturer's instructions. Spoon into a freezer container and freeze for 12 to 16 hours for firm ice cream.

Serves six to eight

VANILLA BEAN GELATO

2   vanilla beans, split
2 1/2 cups heavy cream
3/4   cup sugar
4   eggs

Combine the vanilla beans and cream in a heavy 3-quart saucepan. Bring to a boil over medium heat. Beat the sugar and eggs in a mixing bowl until pale yellow and thick. Stir a small amount of the hot cream into the egg mixture; then stir the egg mixture into the hot cream. Cook over medium heat just until the mixture coats the back of a spoon; do not boil.

Remove from the heat and strain into a medium bowl, reserving the vanilla beans. Place the bowl in a large bowl filled halfway with ice water. Cool the custard until chilled, stirring occasionally. Split the cooled vanilla beans and scrape the seeds into the custard, discarding the pods. Spoon into an ice cream freezer container and freeze using the manufacturer's instructions.

You may chill the custard in the refrigerator for 2 to 8 hours prior to freezing if preferred.

Serves six

CONTRIBUTORS

MANY THANKS TO THE FOLLOWING:

Arlington Hall—location
Jan Barboglio—props
Steve and Diane Carol—location
Camille McBee—wine pairings
Patsy McCutcheon—foreword
Kathy Railsback—food preparation
Dick and Pat Bailey
Ginger Cotton
Todd Fiscus

Donald and Reneé Lawhorne
Raegan McKinney
Claire Moore
Sheri Neumayer
Joan Pursche
Igancio Ramos
Denise Shephard
Nancy Stephenson

MANY THANKS TO THESE PEOPLE WHO CONTRIBUTED RECIPES.
WITHOUT THEM THIS BOOK WOULD NOT HAVE BEEN POSSIBLE.

Sue Adams
Becky Alldredge
Catherine Allen
Margot Anderson
Sheree Armstrong
Betty Ayres
Julie Ayres
Steve Ayres
Pam Barbera
Missy Barlow
Barbara Barndt
Mary Katherine Baxter
Tami Beaton
Diana Benbow
Judy Benedict
Diana Betts
Joan Biggerstaff
Shirley Boesen
Sue Bond
Kathy Boobar
Ann Boswell
Myra Boswell
Shannon Bradshaw
Brandi Bragg
Jill Bramlett
Becky Braud
Jill Brooks
Lorna Brown
Kim Browning
Susan Browning

Janis Buck
Sonya Buehler
Alane Bujko
Diana Burbank
Kathy Burkhalter
Shari Burns
Gay Caldwell
Stephanie Calhoun
Jean Callison
Beverly Carpenter
Carnie Carpenter
Veda Catalano
Sally Cathriner
Brenda Cerrato
Jeri Chambers
Marla Christie
Marthiel Clanton
Shana Clark
Melissa Clayton
Cristi Closs
Jennifer Clutter
Beth Cobb
Jean Cochran
Stacey Cochran
Debra Coffey
Kirsten Colvert
Debbie Coody
Elaine Cook
Stacy Cooper
Cindy Copeland

Jane Coralli
Ginger Elaine Cotton
Mae Crook
Pat Crook
Lisa Crump
Laura Curran
Cathy Curry
Lauren Dana
Anne Deegan
Laurie Dickens
Karen Dilworth
Kimberly Ditore
Kathleen Dockery
Pam Dolberry
Patty Duarte
Rachel Duncan
Donna Dwyer
Elaine Edinger
Rebecca Egelston-Caso
Leslee Engleman
Pat Evans
Carol Fall
Sandra Fay
Martha Feeback
Linda Fennell
Heidi Frederick
Sandi Frost
Laura Furr
Shelia Gilbert
Kristen Gile

Connie Gilliland
Kelly Gonzalez
Lisa Goral
Diane Grefer
Ann Griffin
Sue Griffin
Tanda Griffin
Jodie Grimm
Shannon Grogman
Julie Gunnell
Beth Gustafson
Terri Hagan
Mysti Hale
Ellie T. Hall
Lynne Halydier
Amanda Hamby
Lynn Hanks
Jamie Hanna
Sheryl Harbaugh
Mary Harris
Tisha Harris
Kim Hartwell
Caroline C. Hash
Susan Haslam
Pat Hatchell
Meredith Healey
Sally Keller Herbert
Gerayne Hesseltine
Juanita Holloway
Viola Holloway

Mary Houghton
Kelli Howery
Brenda Hudnall
Stacy Hulin
Tricia Hunsucker
Kelly Hunter
Ronelle Ianace
Sharon Isaly
Nancy Garland Jenison
Diane Jenkins
Steve Johnson
Cheryl Joyner
Geralyn Kaminsky
Frances King
Ginger Kitchens
Beverly Kleckner
Cindy Sue Kolbe
Desiree Lamb
Leno Lewis
Julie Lindberg
Cheryl Litzkow
Kimberly Loftus
Teresa Loftus
Joyce Logan
Jeanne Lowenthal
Joellen Lundquest
Christina Mackey
Marilyn Mahoney
Janet Manchee
Pamela Martinez
Lorraine Mattis
Tamara McCabe
Linda McConnell
Christi McCraw
Ann McKeown
Laurie McMillan
Shirley S. McMillan
Wendy McMillon
Rosalie McShane
Jennifer McWhorter
Deb Merrill
Peggy Michael

Teresa Michelsen
Margie Miller
Zoe Miller
Terri Mitchell
Beverly Moore
Claire Moore
Joa Muns
Jennifer Murray
Anne Neeley
Ginger Neely-Faller
Pat Nelson
Sheri Neumayer
Sabrina Newton
Johanna Nystrom
Jill Oborny
Cissy Oldner
Belinda Orland
Christy Owen
Yolanda Parás
Caren Parrish
Debbie Parsons
Linda Peterson
Lynda Peterson
Jenni Petty
Linda Philhower
Debbie Phillips
Deborah Phillips
Belinda Pittard
Lisa Pladsen
Ruth Plasden
Jennifer Portela
Margie Portela
Cynthia Powell
Martha Presley
Julie Prince
Kathy Prior
Barbara Puchacz
Ina May Pummill
K. C. Pummill
Sue Rackers
Lisa Raskin
Ashley Rasmussen

Barbara Ratliff
Darla Reagin
Pamela Reckler
Melanie Reeh
Leslie Reid
Janet Reierson
Christi Richardson
Victoria Rippner
Lisa Pyle Rodenbaugh
Margaret Rosen
Dolly Rosinki
Angela Rotello
Jennifer Ruhman
Christine Russo
Lisa Sams
Virginia Sanborn
Genevieve Sand
Taura Sanderson
Kathy Schell
Helga Schumacher
Lisa Caudill Schumacher
Agnes Schwalm
Mary Anne Seale
Dana Serafine
Betty Seymour
Beth Shanafelt
Florence Shapiro
Denise Shepard
Nancy Simmons
Leigh Slade
Brenda Small
Harolyn Hodges
Lu Smith
Allyson Spindler
Susan Spindler
Heather Sprock
Kaye St. Peter
Kerry Stallman
Sue Stark
Sheri Steele
Vicki Stone
Kindra Strachan

Shawn Stratman
Spencer Stratman
Melynda Swann
Martha Teague
Amy Thompson
Carol Thompson
Nancy Thompson
Lisa Toohey
Sherri Trinler
Debbie Tschetter
Mandy Tschoepe
Jennifer Van Arsdel
Sydney VanRoekel
Betty Veale
Amy Velasquez
Terri Lowenstein Wagner
Tracy Wallner
Heather Weemes
Kim Weiner
Beth Weingarden
Sabre Weis
Melanie Welch
Roseann Whieldon
Sue Whieldon
Kay White
Janice Whitehill
Julee Greeson Williams
Cathy Wilson
Kathy Wilson
Melissa Woods
Anita Wormald
Cindy Worth
Brandi Wright
Kathy Yonts
Shyla Yosten
Dee Young
Laura Young
Liz Farris
Holly Howe
Marian Lokey

INDEX

LONE STAR TO FIVE STAR
Culinary Creations for Every Occasion

The Junior League of Plano
5805 Coit Road, Suite 301
Plano, Texas 75093
1-888-368-STAR
FAX: 972-769-2229
WWW.JLPlano.org

YOUR ORDER	QUANTITY	TOTAL
LONE STAR TO FIVE STAR at $26.95 per book		$
Postage and handling at $4.50 per book		$
	TOTAL	$

Name

Address

City   State   Zip

Telephone

Method of Payment: [   ] MasterCard   [   ] VISA
                      [   ] Check payable to Junior League of Plano

Account Number   Expiration Date

Signature

Note: Prices subject to change without notice.

Photocopies will be accepted.